GRADE 4

240 Vocabulary Words Kids Need to Know

24 Ready-to-Reproduce Packets
That Make
Vocabulary Building
Fun & Effective

by Linda Ward Beech

SCHOLASTIC
Teaching
Resources

New York • Toronto • London • Auckland • Sydney
Mexico City • New Delhi • Hong Kong • Buenos Aires

Cover design by Gerard Fuchs

Interior design by Melinda Belter

Interior illustrations by Steve Cox, Mike Moran

ISBN: 0-439-28044-3

9 10   40   09 08

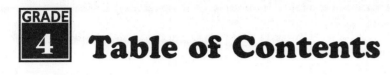

Table of Contents

Using the Book

Where would we be without words? It's hard to imagine. Words are a basic building block of communication, and a strong vocabulary is an essential part of reading, writing, and speaking well. The purpose of this book is to help learners expand the number of words they know and the ways in which they use them. Although 240 vocabulary words are introduced, many more words and meanings are woven into the book's 24 lessons.

Learning new words is not just about encountering them; it's about using, exploring, and thinking about them. So the lessons in this book are organized around different aspects and attributes of words—related meanings, how words are formed, where words come from, coined words, homophones, homographs, word parts, clips, blends, and much more. The lessons provide an opportunity for students to try out words and to reflect and have fun with them.

Materials: As you introduce the lessons, be sure to have the following items available:

> **dictionaries**
> **thesauruses**
> **writing notebooks or journals**
> **writing tools**

TIP You'll find a complete alphabetized list of all the lesson words at the back of the book.

Lesson Organization: Each lesson is three pages long and introduces ten words.

The first lesson page includes:

lesson words

statement of lesson focus

simple sentences explaining the meanings of the words

two exercises

The second page includes:

lesson words

cloze activity

thinking activity with test prep fill-ins

Writing to Learn component

The third page includes:

puzzle, game, or other learning activity using the words

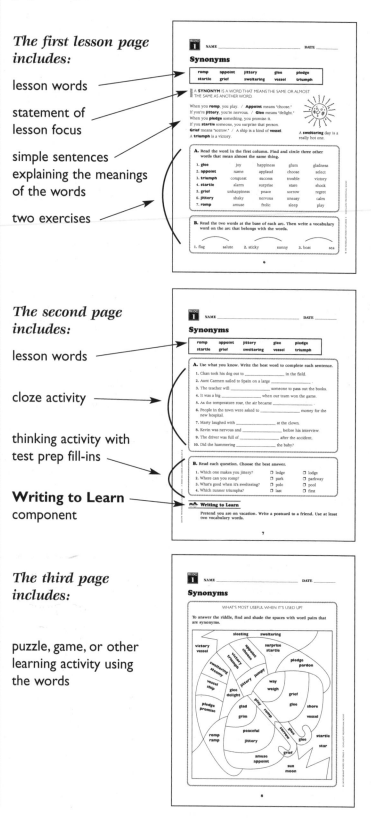

Tips for Using the Lessons

- Many words have more than one meaning, including some that are not given in the lesson. You may want to point out additional meanings or invite students to discover them independently.

- Many words can be used as more than one part of speech. Again, you can expand students' vocabulary by drawing attention to such usage.

- Have students complete the Writing to Learn activities in a notebook or journal so they have a specific place where they can refer to and review words.

- Consider having students make a set of word cards for each lesson, or make a class set and place it in your writing center.

- Build word family lists with words based on major phonograms such as *fret, chide,* or *vain.*

- Don't hesitate to add your own writing assignments. The more students use a word, the more likely they are to "own" it.

- Be aware of pronunciation differences when teaching homographs. Not all students may pronounce words in the same way, and this can lead to confusion.

- Use the words to teach syllabication rules.

- Use the words to teach related spelling and grammar rules.

- Encourage students to make semantic maps for some words. For instance, they might organize a map for a noun to show what the word is, what it is like, what it is not like, and include examples of the word.

- Have students illustrate some words.

- Help students make connections by pointing out lesson words used in other contexts and materials.

- Discuss other forms of a word, for example *loyal, loyalty, disloyal, loyalist.* Encourage students to word build in this fashion.

- Have students categorize words.

- Encourage students to consult more than one reference and to compare information.

TIP Consider having students fill out Word Inventory Sheets before each lesson. The headings for such a sheet might be: Words I Know; Words I Have Seen but Don't Really Know; New Words. Using pencils, students can list the vocabulary words and probable meanings under the headings. As the lesson proceeds, they can make revisions and additions.

Synonyms

romp	appoint	jittery	glee	pledge
startle	grief	sweltering	vessel	triumph

█ A **SYNONYM** IS A WORD THAT MEANS THE SAME OR ALMOST
THE SAME AS ANOTHER WORD.

When you **romp**, you play. / **Appoint** means "choose."

If you're **jittery**, you're nervous. / **Glee** means "delight."

When you **pledge** something, you promise it.

If you **startle** someone, you surprise that person.

Grief means "sorrow." / A ship is a kind of **vessel**.

A **triumph** is a victory.

A **sweltering** day is a really hot one.

A. Read the word in the first column. Find and circle three other
words that mean almost the same thing.

1. **glee**	joy	happiness	(glum)	gladness
2. **appoint**	name	applaud	(choose)	select
3. **triumph**	conquest	success	trouble	(victory)
4. **startle**	alarm	(surprise)	stare	shock
5. **grief**	unhappiness	peace	(sorrow)	regret
6. **jittery**	shaky	(nervous)	uneasy	calm
7. **romp**	amuse	frolic	sleep	(play)

B. Read the two words at the base of each arc. Then write a vocabulary
word on the arc that belongs with the words.

sweltering   _vessel_

⌒   ⌒   ⌒

1. flag   salute   **2.** sticky   sunny   **3.** boat   sea

Synonyms

~~romp~~	appoint	jittery	glee	pledge
startle	grief	sweltering	vessel	triumph

A. Use what you know. Write the best word to complete each sentence.

1. Chan took his dog out to _romp_ in the field.

2. Aunt Carmen sailed to Spain on a large _vessel_ .

3. The teacher will _Appoint_ someone to pass out the books.

4. It was a big _____ when our team won the game.

5. As the temperature rose, the air became _Sweltering_ .

6. People in the town were asked to _____ money for the new hospital.

7. Marty laughed with _Glee_ at the clown.

8. Kevin was nervous and _Jittery_ before his interview.

9. The driver was full of _____ after the accident.

10. Did the hammering _____ the baby?

B. Read each question. Choose the best answer.

1. Which one makes you jittery? ❑ ledge ❑ lodge
2. Where can you romp? ☑ park ❑ parkway
3. What's good when it's sweltering? ❑ polo ☑ pool
4. Which runner triumphs? ❑ last ☑ first

✏️ Writing to Learn

Pretend you are on vacation. Write a postcard to a friend. Use at least two vocabulary words.

NAME _____   DATE _____

Synonyms

WHAT'S MOST USEFUL WHEN IT'S USED UP?

To answer the riddle, find and shade the spaces with word pairs that are synonyms.

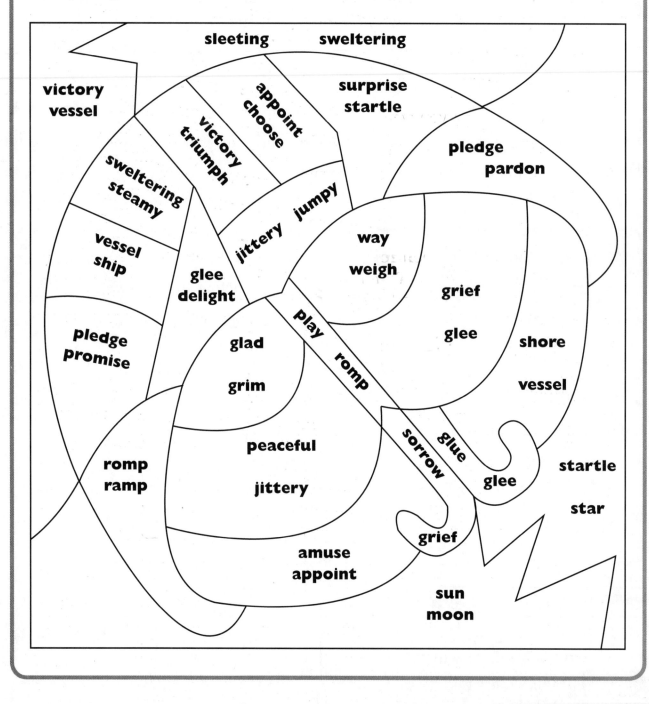

Synonyms

unfurl	thaw	din	garment	chide
vast	nimble	trophy	eerie	fret

A **SYNONYM** IS A WORD THAT MEANS THE SAME OR ALMOST THE SAME AS ANOTHER WORD.

If you **unfurl** something, you unfold it.

When ice **thaws**, it melts. / A **din** is a loud noise.

A **garment** is something you wear.

If you **chide** someone, you scold that person.

Vast means "great." / **Nimble** means "quick."

A **trophy** is a prize. / When you **fret**, you worry.

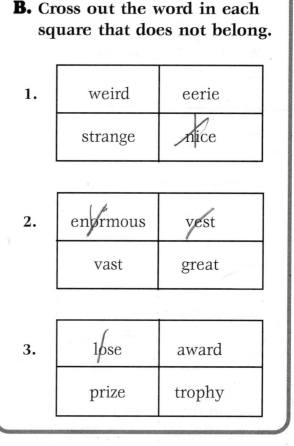

Eerie means "strange."

A. Read the words in each row. Write a vocabulary word that means almost the same thing.

1. unfold, open _Unfurl_

2. vex, trouble _chide_

3. racket, uproar _din_

4. scold, nag _chide_

5. brisk, quick _Nimble_

6. dissolve, melt _thaw_

7. clothing, apparel _garment_

B. Cross out the word in each square that does not belong.

1.

weird	eerie
strange	~~nice~~

2.

~~enormous~~	~~vest~~
vast	great

3.

~~lose~~	award
prize	trophy

Synonyms

unfurl	thaw	din	garment	chide
vast	nimble	trophy	eerie	fret

A. Use what you know. Write the best word to complete each sentence.

1. The heads of state all met in a _____ hall.

2. We watched the flag _____ in the breeze.

3. The actor wore a purple _____ in the play.

4. Our dog won a _____ at the pet show.

5. Mom will _____ you for leaving the window open.

6. The ice began to _____ in the warm sun.

7. Bart's rock band made a _____ when they practiced.

8. A _____ cat ran along the top of the fence.

9. When Dad was late, Sonny began to _____ .

10. It was _____ inside the empty building.

B. Read each question. Choose the best answer.

1. When does it thaw?   ❏ spring   ❏ fall
2. What makes a din?   ❏ clatter   ❏ whisper
3. Which ones unfurl?   ❏ petals   ❏ pedals
4. Which one can you wear? ❏ garment   ❏ garden

✏ Writing to Learn

Design a new item of clothing. Then write a description of it. Use at least two vocabulary words.

Synonyms

Write a vocabulary word that is a synonym for each word in the list.
Then use the words to help you get through the maze.

1. creepy   _____   6. great   _____

2. worry   _____   7. award   _____

3. scold   _____   8. noise   _____

4. dress   _____   9. open   _____

5. quick   _____   10. melt   _____

Start   End

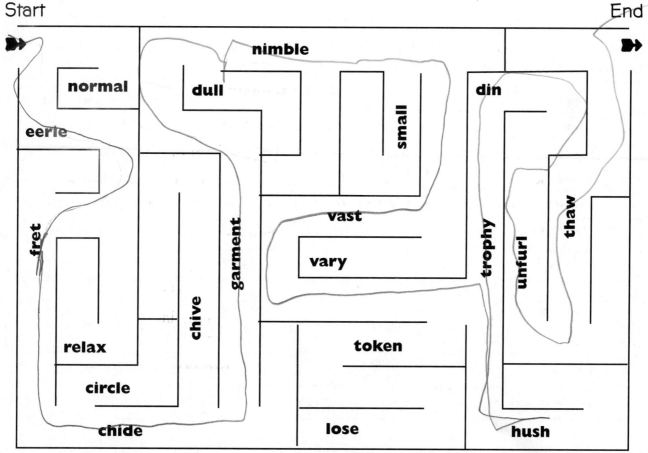

Antonyms

native	excited	dissimilar	reduce	appear
foreign	calm	identical	enlarge	vanish

AN **ANTONYM** IS A WORD THAT MEANS THE OPPOSITE OF ANOTHER WORD.

A **native** plant is from here, while a **foreign** plant comes from someplace else.

If you get too **excited**, you need to **calm** down.

Things that are not **identical** are **dissimilar**.

Enlarge means "to make things bigger," and **reduce** means "to make things smaller."

The clouds made the sun **vanish**, but when they moved, the sun would **appear** again.

We're identical.

We're just the same.

A. Read the word in the first column. Find and circle the word that has the opposite meaning.

1. **excited**   upset   ~~relaxed~~   exercise
2. **identical**   identity   similar   different
3. **foreign**   unknown   native   forest
4. **vanish**   depart   disappear   reveal
5. **reduce**   magnify   lessen   redo
6. **dissimilar**   unique   alike   distant
7. **native**   domestic   original   alien

B. Read the words in each box. Write the two words that are antonyms.

1.

stirred	beautiful
calm		

_____

_____

2.

appear	appeal
leave		

_____

_____

3.

decrease	enlarge
enrage		

_____

_____

NAME _____ **DATE** _____

Antonyms

native	excited	dissimilar	reduce	appear
foreign	calm	identical	enlarge	vanish

A. Use what you know. Write the best word to complete each sentence.

1. Let's _____ the photo so it fits in this big frame.

2. No two people have _____ fingerprints.

3. The clerk couldn't understand the customers who spoke in a _____ language.

4. Without any wind, the sea remained smooth and _____ .

5. Although Syd and Ali come from _____ backgrounds, they are good friends.

6. Turn on the TV, and a picture will _____ .

7. Nan got very _____ after hearing the good news.

8. It's best to put in plants that are _____ to this area.

9. If I give up snacks, I can _____ my expenses.

10. We waved goodbye and watched the car _____ down the road.

B. Read each question. Choose the best answer.

1. Which one is foreign? ❏ Italian ❏ English
2. Which ones are identical? ❏ cousins ❏ twins
3. What is a cheerleader? ❏ calm ❏ excited
4. Which one reduces? ❏ addition ❏ subtraction

Writing to Learn

Write an ad for a household product. Use at least two vocabulary words in your ad.

Antonyms

Rewrite Lucy's letter to her sister. Use an antonym for each underlined word.

Dear Barb,

When I woke up, you were gone. How could you just <u>appear</u> like that? I wish you weren't going to school in a <u>native</u> country. It seems so far away.

Dad and I are going to <u>reduce</u> the garden this year. I'm very <u>calm</u> because there will be more room for flowers. We will put in some new things and some that are <u>dissimilar</u> to what we've had before. You'll be pleased when you return.

Love,

Lucy

_____

_____

_____

_____

_____

_____

© 240 VOCABULARY WORDS FOR GRADE 4 • SCHOLASTIC PROFESSIONAL BOOKS

NAME _____ DATE _____

Antonyms

collect	torrent	maintain	snare	methodical
disperse	trickle	discontinue	release	haphazard

▌ AN **ANTONYM** IS A WORD THAT MEANS
THE OPPOSITE OF ANOTHER WORD.

This is no **trickle**; this is a **torrent**!

Collect means "to gather," and **disperse** means "to give out."

Maintain means "to keep something," and **discontinue** means "to stop it."

When you **snare** something, you catch it, but when you **release** something, you let it go.

A neat person is **methodical**, while a messy person is **haphazard**.

A. Read each word in the first column. Draw a line to match it with an antonym in the second column.

1. **trickle**   a. drip
2. **methodical**   b. stop
3. **torrent**   c. sloppy
4. **maintain**   d. continue
5. **haphazard**   e. flood
6. **discontinue**   f. tidy

B. Read each word in the first column. Underline the word that is an antonym. Circle the word that is a synonym.

1. **snare**   a. capture   b. release   c. share
2. **collect** a. collection b. assemble   c. disperse
3. **release** a. free   b. review   c. grab
4. **disperse** a. college   b. distribute c. gather

NAME _____ DATE _____

Antonyms

collect	torrent	maintain	snare	methodical
disperse	trickle	discontinue	release	haphazard

A. Use what you know. Write the best word to complete each sentence.

1. The dog would not _____ its hold on the bone.

2. Ben files things in an orderly and _____ way.

3. Di likes to _____ dolls from other countries.

4. When the creek overflowed, a _____ of water poured over the bank.

5. In the game, we had to _____ a fish with a magnet.

6. The messy shelves were piled with stuff in a _____ way.

7. When Dad shut off the hose, a small _____ of water ran out.

8. They will _____ free tickets at the door of the concert hall.

9. Nina tries to _____ her bike in good working order.

10. Because of poor sales, the company will _____ that line of shirts.

B. Read each question. Choose the best answer.

1. Which one can snare? ❏ trip ❏ trap
2. Which one is dangerous? ❏ haphazard ❏ careful
3. Which one can trickle? ❏ muffin ❏ milk
4. What does a conductor do? ❏ collect ❏ distribute

✐ Writing to Learn

Write three headlines for newspaper stories. Use at least three vocabulary words.

Antonyms

Play tic-tac-antonym. Read each word. Then draw a line through three words in the box that are antonyms for that word. Your line can be vertical, horizontal, or diagonal.

1. discontinue

stop	keep	share
move	maintain	distract
lost	preserve	shorten

2. collect

correct	collar	assemble
call	gather	column
distribute	scatter	disperse

3. methodical

careless	slippery	method
happily	haphazard	orderly
neat	careful	unorganized

4. torrent

flood	tickle	dribble
current	torture	trickle
tornado	trouble	drip

5. release

snare	trap	capture
scoop	retreat	free
snarl	relay	unfasten

Compound Words

driftwood	**water**front	**card**board	**junk**yard	**sun**burn
beanstalk	**quick**sand	**text**book	**land**mark	**ginger**bread

A **COMPOUND WORD** IS A WORD MADE UP OF TWO SMALLER WORDS PUT TOGETHER.

Wood that floats on water is **driftwood**.

Land along a body of water is a **waterfront**.

Cardboard is stiff, heavy paper.

A **junkyard** is where junk is kept.

If you get too much sun, you have a **sunburn**.

The stalk on which beans grow is a **beanstalk**.

You use a **textbook** to learn about a subject.

Quicksand is loose sand and water that gives way under weight.

A **landmark** is a building or place kept to mark an event that happened there.

Gingerbread is a kind of cake or cookie made with ginger.

A. Complete each sentence with a vocabulary word.

1. Sand that sinks quickly is _____ .

2. A stalk for a bean is a _____ .

3. A book full of text is a _____ .

4. Land that fronts on water is a

_____ .

5. Wood that drifts in water is

_____ .

6. A burn from the sun is a _____ .

7. A yard full of junk is a _____ .

B. Write the two words that make up each compound word.

1. **landmark**

_____

_____

2. **cardboard**

_____

_____

3. **gingerbread**

_____

_____

NAME _____ DATE _____

Compound Words

driftwood	**water**front	**card**board	**junk**yard	**sun**burn
beanstalk	**quick**sand	**text**book	**land**mark	**ginger**bread

A. Use what you know. Write the best word to complete each sentence.

1. Verna got a bad _____ at the beach.

2. That box is made of _____ .

3. Don't step on the _____ or you'll sink.

4. For today's assignment, you need your science _____ .

5. Pieces of _____ floated to the shore.

6. The cottage was on the _____ with a view of the sea.

7. Mrs. Banks made _____ for the class party.

8. In the story, Jack climbed up a _____ .

9. There are a lot of old cars at the _____ .

10. That church is a _____ because of what happened there.

B. Read each question. Choose the best answer.

1. Which one is a plant?   ❑ beanbag   ❑ beanstalk
2. Which one is historic?   ❑ landfill   ❑ landmark
3. Which one hurts?   ❑ sunburn   ❑ sunset
4. Which one is a place?   ❑ junkyard   ❑ jumpstart

Writing to Learn

Write a sign for a landmark, waterfront, or junkyard. Use at least one other vocabulary word on the sign.

Compound Words

The compound words are mixed up. Use the clues to rewrite each word so it is correct.

1. **textsand**   a book for learning   _____

2. **sunstalk**   too much sun   _____

3. **waterwood**   down by the sea   _____

4. **quickfront**   dangerous soil   _____

5. **landbread**   a place to remember   _____

6. **gingerburn**   a tasty treat   _____

7. **beanmark**   a vegetable stem   _____

8. **cardyard**   heavy paper   _____

9. **junkbook**   a scrap heap   _____

10. **driftboard**   floating branches   _____

Homophones

boar	sweet	vein	metal	boulder
bore	suite	vain	mettle	bolder

A **HOMOPHONE** IS A WORD THAT SOUNDS LIKE ANOTHER WORD BUT HAS A DIFFERENT MEANING AND A DIFFERENT SPELLING.

A **boar** is a wild pig.
An uninteresting person can be a **bore.**

Sugar and honey taste **sweet**.
A **suite** is a group of rooms that are connected.
Someone who is **vain** is proud.

Mettle is courage. / A **metal** is a substance such as iron, copper, silver, lead, or brass.

A **boulder** is a big rock. / When you feel braver, you feel **bolder**.

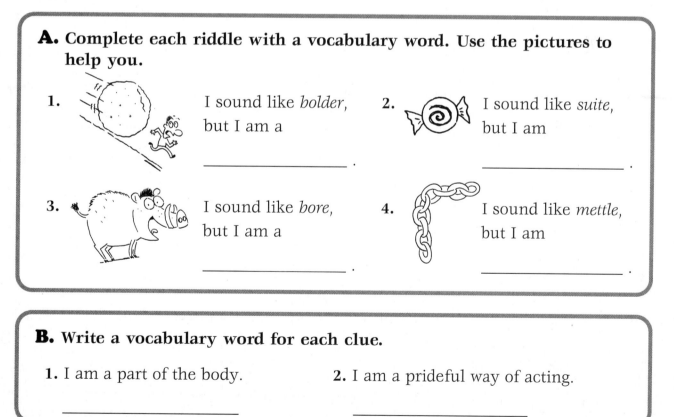

A **vein** is a vessel that carries blood to your heart.

A. Complete each riddle with a vocabulary word. Use the pictures to help you.

1. I sound like *bolder*, but I am a _____ .

2. I sound like *suite*, but I am _____ .

3. I sound like *bore*, but I am a _____ .

4. I sound like *mettle*, but I am _____ .

B. Write a vocabulary word for each clue.

1. I am a part of the body.   2. I am a prideful way of acting.

_____   _____

Homophones

boar	sweet	vein	metal	boulder
bore	suite	vain	mettle	bolder

A. Use what you know. Write the best word to complete each sentence.

1. Our family rented a _____ of rooms at the hotel.

2. We climbed over a huge _____ on the hike.

3. Greg really showed his _____ during the storm.

4. The singer was rather _____ about his fine voice.

5. Dad always likes something _____ for dessert.

6. After she improved, Delia felt _____ about speaking French.

7. Much of a car is made from _____ .

8. The speaker was such a _____ that Hal fell asleep.

9. The runner could feel the blood pumping through his _____ .

10. A _____ has bristles and lives in the woods.

B. Read each question. Choose the best answer.

1. Which one is sweet? ❏ gumdrop ❏ lemon
2. What's made of metal? ❏ spoon ❏ soup
3. Which one is dull? ❏ boar ❏ bore
4. Which one's a boulder? ❏ rock ❏ pebble

Writing to Learn

Use a pair of the homophones to write a riddle.

Homophones

These book titles have errors in them. Rewrite each title so it is correct.

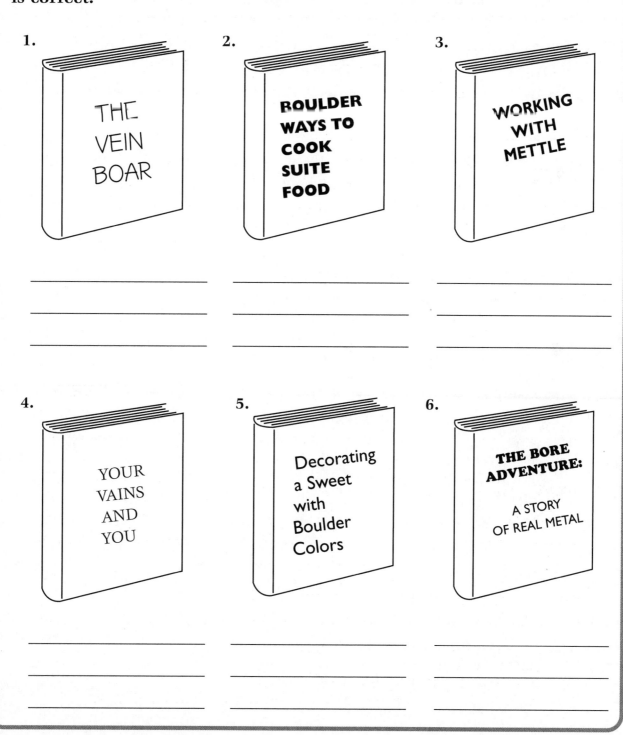

1.

THE
VEIN
BOAR

_____
_____
_____

2.

BOULDER
WAYS TO
COOK
SUITE
FOOD

_____
_____
_____

3.

WORKING
WITH
METTLE

_____
_____
_____

4.

YOUR
VAINS
AND
YOU

_____
_____
_____

5.

Decorating
a Sweet
with
Boulder
Colors

_____
_____
_____

6.

THE BORE
ADVENTURE:

A STORY
OF REAL METAL

_____
_____
_____

Homographs

prune	**desert**	**grouse**	**bass**	**sewer**
prune	desert	grouse	bass	sewer

A **HOMOGRAPH** IS A WORD THAT IS SPELLED THE SAME AS ANOTHER WORD BUT HAS A DIFFERENT MEANING AND SOMETIMES A DIFFERENT PRONUNCIATION.

A **prune** is a dried plum.
When you **prune** something, you trim it.
If you **desert** someone, you leave that person.
A **desert** is a region with little rainfall.
A **grouse** is a kind of bird.
A **bass** is a kind of fish.
The low singing voice of a man is a **bass**.
Someone who sews is a **sewer**. / A **sewer** is a pipe for carrying away waste.

If you **grouse**, you complain.

A. Read each sentence. Then circle the correct word.

1. This lake has a lot of **bass**.   **a.** bas   **b.** bās
2. This cactus grows in the **desert**.   **a.** de' zert   **b.** di 'zert
3. A **sewer** made this dress.   **a.** sō' er   **b.** soo' er
4. We hoped the guide wouldn't **desert** us.   **a.** dez' ert   **b.** di 'zurt
5. The **sewer** in our town runs beneath the ground. **a.** sō' er   **b.** soo' er
6. The **bass** singer in the chorus was good.   **a.** bas   **b.** bās

B. Write a vocabulary word for each underlined word or words.

1. The gardener will <u>clip</u> the bushes.   _____

2. We saw a <u>bird</u> flying overhead.   _____

3. The boys will <u>grumble</u> if they miss the show.   _____

4. A <u>dried plum</u> is a good snack.   _____

Homographs

prune	desert	grouse	bass	sewer
prune	desert	grouse	bass	sewer

A. Use what you know. Write the best word to complete each sentence.

1. It's not fair to _____ the team now.

2. If you _____ the tree, you'll have a better view.

3. No one wants to hear you _____ all the time.

4. It's usually very warm in the _____ during the day.

5. Every street has a _____ for waste.

6. Nelson caught a _____ in the river.

7. A musical instrument with low tones is the _____ fiddle.

8. Look at all the _____ on the branches of that tree.

9. Mom is a good _____ and will make my costume.

10. If you want some fruit, there is one _____ left in the box.

B. Read each question. Choose the best answer.

1. Can a grouse grouse?   ❏ yes   ❏ no

2. Does a bass sing bass?   ❏ yes   ❏ no

3. Can you desert a desert?   ❏ yes   ❏ no

4. Does a sewer need a sewer?   ❏ yes   ❏ no

Writing to Learn

Explain why homographs can be confusing. Give some tips for understanding them. Use at least two vocabulary words as examples.

NAME _____ DATE _____

Homographs

Shade each word in Column 1 a different color. Then find one meaning of the word in Column 2 and another meaning in Column 3. Color the meanings to match the word in the first column.

	COLUMN I	COLUMN 2	COLUMN 3
1.	**sewer**	a dry region	a dried fruit
2.	**grouse**	a plump bird	to flee from something
3.	**desert**	a large underground channel	to grumble and fuss
4.	**bass**	to cut back plants	a person who uses a needle and thread
5.	**prune**	a fish that is good to eat	a drum with a low tone

Eponyms

braille	sandwich	saxophone	bloomers	tweed
guppy	titanic	Ferris wheel	limerick	jovial

▎AN **EPONYM** IS A WORD THAT COMES FROM THE NAME OF A PERSON OR PLACE.

A **Ferris wheel** has seats hanging from a large wheel that turns.

Braille is a system of writing with raised dots for blind people.

A **sandwich** is two pieces of bread with a filling between them.

The **saxophone** is a musical instrument.

Bloomers are long pants gathered at the knee.

Tweed is a woolen cloth made with two or more colors of yarn.

A **guppy** is a small, colorful fish. / **Titanic** means "huge or great."

A **limerick** is a funny five-line poem. / If someone is **jovial**, that person is jolly.

A. Write a vocabulary word for each sentence.

1. John Montagu, the Earl of Sandwich, ate meat between bread to save time. _____

2. Limerick is a place in Ireland named in a popular poem. _____

3. Antoine Sax invented a brass instrument. _____

4. George Ferris invented a new ride for a fair in 1893. _____

5. R.J.L. Guppy brought some fish from the West Indies to England. _____

6. Louis Braille made it possible for blind people to read. _____

B. Draw a line to match each word with its name story.

1. **jovial**   a. Amelia Bloomer started a fad of wearing loose trousers under her dress.

2. **titanic**   b. This wool was made beside the Tweed River in Scotland.

3. **tweed**   c. Jove was a Roman god also called Jupiter.

4. **bloomers**   d. The Titans were powerful Greek gods.

Eponyms

braille	sandwich	saxophone	bloomers	tweed
guppy	titanic	Ferris wheel	limerick	jovial

A. Use what you know. Write the best word to complete each sentence.

1. Ed wore his new _____ jacket to the meeting.

2. The clown's _____ face made us laugh.

3. This library has a section of books printed in _____ .

4. On Poetry Day, Abe read a funny _____ to the class.

5. The doll in the window had on white _____ beneath her dress.

6. Charlie "Bird" Parker was a famous _____ player.

7. Peanut butter and jelly is my favorite _____ .

8. Lee got a brightly colored _____ for her fish tank.

9. It took a _____ effort to carry the couch upstairs.

10. We rode on a _____ at the state fair.

B. Read each question. Choose the best answer.

1. Which one is jovial?   ❑ winner   ❑ loser
2. Which one is warmer?   ❑ cotton   ❑ tweed
3. Which one has fins?   ❑ guppy   ❑ puppy
4. Which one's for lunch?   ❑ sandbox   ❑ sandwich

✎ Writing to Learn

Find out more about the person or place related to a vocabulary word. Write a paragraph to report on your information.

Eponyms

Read each clue. Then find and circle each word in the puzzle. Write the word next to its clue.

```
C  Y  O  L  R  M  F  B  X  T  D  P  G
K  U  G  N  J  S  P  L  H  F  Q  J  I
A  S  A  X  O  P  H  O  N  E  C  Y  S
W  A  F  U  V  Y  A  O  L  R  E  H  W
J  N  M  E  I  L  I  M  E  R  I  C  K
P  D  T  O  A  G  R  E  J  I  Z  L  F
B  W  Z  I  L  U  N  R  A  S  O  X  G
T  I  T  A  N  I  C  S  Q  W  K  I  U
U  C  N  K  C  O  M  G  Z  H  M  B  P
Q  H  T  Y  J  S  N  Y  V  E  C  V  P
A  F  P  F  N  L  T  W  E  E  D  S  Y
V  M  X  E  B  R  A  I  L  L  E  T  E
```

1. It makes music.   _____

2. It has rhyme.   _____

3. great strength   _____

4. colorful wool cloth   _____

5. a special alphabet   _____

6. bread and filling   _____

7. cheerful   _____

8. garment for legs   _____

9. spinning wheel   _____

10. swimming pet   _____

Words From Other Languages

mustang	patio	caboose	sleigh	ski
avocado	rodeo	waffle	yacht	skull

MANY WORDS IN ENGLISH COME FROM **OTHER LANGUAGES**.

Ski is a Danish word for a long flat runner worn on the foot.

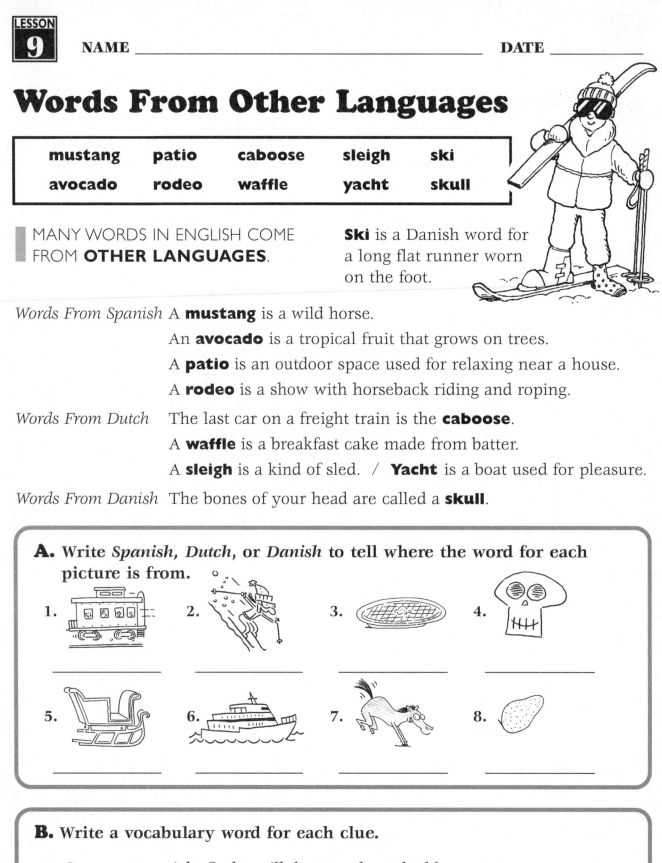

Words From Spanish A **mustang** is a wild horse.

An **avocado** is a tropical fruit that grows on trees.

A **patio** is an outdoor space used for relaxing near a house.

A **rodeo** is a show with horseback riding and roping.

Words From Dutch The last car on a freight train is the **caboose**.

A **waffle** is a breakfast cake made from batter.

A **sleigh** is a kind of sled. / **Yacht** is a boat used for pleasure.

Words From Danish The bones of your head are called a **skull**.

A. Write *Spanish, Dutch,* or *Danish* to tell where the word for each picture is from.

1. _____   2. _____   3. _____   4. _____

5. _____   6. _____   7. _____   8. _____

B. Write a vocabulary word for each clue.

1. On me, you might find a grill, hammock, and table. _____

2. At me, you might find a lasso, bronco, and bull. _____

© 240 VOCABULARY WORDS FOR GRADE 4 SCHOLASTIC PROFESSIONAL BOOKS

NAME _____   DATE _____

Words From Other Languages

mustang	patio	caboose	sleigh	ski
avocado	rodeo	waffle	yacht	skull

A. Use what you know. Write the best word to complete each sentence.

1. Your brain is protected by your _____ .

2. At the end of the train was the _____ .

3. We went for a _____ ride in the snow.

4. The pit of an _____ is very large.

5. Nick ordered a _____ and bacon for breakfast.

6. The wild _____ galloped across the plains.

7. Juan fell while getting off the lift and lost a _____ .

8. The guests went for a sunset sail on the _____ .

9. The cowboys headed for the _____ to show off their skills.

10. In the summer, our neighbors eat supper on their _____ .

B. Read each question. Choose the best answer.

1. Which one is green?   ❑ waffle   ❑ avocado
2. Which one has wheels?   ❑ sleigh   ❑ caboose
3. Which come in pairs?   ❑ skis   ❑ yachts
4. Which one do you watch?   ❑ radio   ❑ rodeo

Writing to Learn

Pretend you are a travel agent. Write a brochure telling customers about things they might see and do on a vacation. Use at least two vocabulary words.

NAME _____ **DATE** _____

Words From Other Languages

Here are ten questions to make you think.

1. How are a skull and an avocado skin alike? _____

_____

2. What can you do on both a patio and a yacht? _____

_____

3. What do sleighs and skis have in common? _____

_____

4. What relationship is there between a waffle and an avocado? _____

_____

5. How are a yacht and a sleigh similar? _____

_____

6. What relationship is there between a mustang and a rodeo? _____

_____

7. In what way are a caboose and a yacht alike? _____

_____

8. When might an avocado appear on a patio? _____

_____

9. What relationship is there between a mustang and a skull? _____

_____

10. Why might a waffle appear on a yacht? _____

_____

Words From Other Languages

gong	umbrella	opera	judo	depot
paddy	ravioli	trampoline	futon	corduroy

MANY WORDS IN ENGLISH COME FROM **OTHER LANGUAGES**.

Words From French   A **depot** is a station or storehouse.

Corduroy is a cotton cloth with ridges.

Words From Malay   A **paddy** is a flooded field where rice grows.

A **gong** is a kind of bell that makes a deep sound when struck.

Words From Italian   An **umbrella** protects you from rain or sun.

Ravioli is a small pocket of pasta filled with meat or cheese.

An **opera** is a story performed in song and music.

Words From Japanese   **Judo** is a sport and form of self-defense using the body.

A **futon** is a kind of mattress.

Trampoline is an Italian word.

A. Write *French, Malay, Italian,* or *Japanese* to tell where the word for each picture is from.

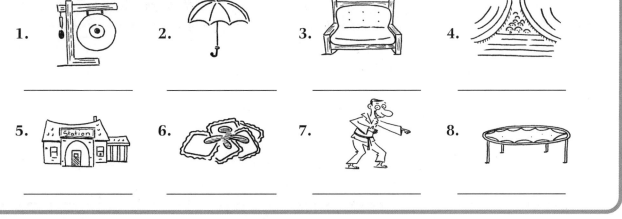

1. _____   2. _____   3. _____   4. _____

5. _____   6. _____   7. _____   8. _____

B. Write a vocabulary word for each clue.

1. Many people eat the grain that comes from me. _____

2. People wear pants and jackets made of me. _____

Words From Other Languages

gong	umbrella	opera	judo	depot
paddy	ravioli	trampoline	futon	corduroy

A. Use what you know. Write the best word to complete each sentence.

1. Meg slept on a _____ when she visited Dale.

2. You'll need an _____ today because it's raining.

3. When the _____ was rung, the campers went to dinner.

4. The acrobats did flips while jumping on the _____ .

5. Jody showed us some of the moves she learned in _____ .

6. As the curtain rose, the audience settled in to watch the _____ .

7. Farmers build a low dirt wall to hold water in the rice _____ .

8. The little boy wore brown _____ overalls.

9. Uncle Pete was waiting at the _____ for our bus.

10. One of Janet's favorite foods is _____ .

B. Read each question. Choose the best answer.

1. Which sound does a gong make? ❏ bing ❏ bong
2. Which one's like a paddy? ❏ puddle ❏ paddle
3. Which one do you stop at? ❏ depot ❏ detour
4. What's a trampoline for? ❏ trembling ❏ tumbling

Writing to Learn

Pretend you are a set designer. Describe a set for an opera or play that you are designing. Use at least three vocabulary words.

Words From Other Languages

Read each list of words. Write a vocabulary word to go with each group.

1. _____

     chorus

     costume

     orchestra

2. _____

     sleep

     rest

     nap

3. _____

     bounce

     jump

     high

4. _____

     sun

     rain

     open

5. _____

     stop

     wait

     go

6. _____

     cheese

     sauce

     pasta

7. _____

     defend

     movement

     attack

8. _____

     bell

     buzzer

     noise

9. _____

     cloth

     cotton

     bumpy

10. _____

     plant

     weed

     harvest

Clips

deli	disco	vet	gym	dorm
condo	mayo	gas	flu	drape

▌ A **CLIP** IS A WORD THAT HAS BEEN
SHORTENED, OR CLIPPED.

A **deli** is a store that sells prepared foods.

A **disco** is a nightclub where people go to dance.

If your pet is sick, you take it to a **vet**.

A **gym** is a place for sports and exercise.

Students sleep in a **dorm** at school.

In a **condo**, a person owns an apartment instead of renting it.

Mayo is a sauce that people use on sandwiches and salads.

A clip for *gasoline* is **gas.**   /   You put a **drape** over a window.

The **flu** is an illness that causes high temperatures and aches.

A. Draw a line to match each clip to the word from which it comes.

1. **disco**   a. gasoline

2. **drape**   b. delicatessen

3. **gas**   c. condominium

4. **vet**   d. gymnasium

5. **condo**   e. drapery

6. **deli**   f. discotheque

7. **gym**   g. veterinarian

B. Write the clip for each word.

1. mayonnaise   2. dormitory   3. influenza

_____   _____   _____

Clips

deli	disco	vet	gym	dorm
condo	mayo	gas	flu	drape

A. Use what you know. Write the best word to complete each sentence.

1. Bill lives in a _____ at college.

2. Please add some _____ to that tuna fish sandwich.

3. Lewis pulled open the _____ so he could see the view.

4. The workers stopped at the _____ to pick up some lunch.

5. Many students play basketball in the school _____

6. Our teacher has been absent because she has the _____

7. Mr. Perez got out of his car to pump _____

8. The Tylers are buying a _____ in this building.

9. The _____, Dr. Singh, examined my cat.

10. Lily goes dancing at a _____ with friends.

B. Read each question. Choose the best answer.

1. Which one is a home?   ❒ disco   ❒ condo
2. Which one causes fever?   ❒ flue   ❒ flu
3. Which one is a doctor?   ❒ pet   ❒ vet
4. Which one's a deli?   ❒ shop   ❒ ship

Writing to Learn

Write three sentences about jobs that people do. Use a vocabulary word in each sentence.

Clips

Complete a chain for each word. In each circle, write a word that is
related to the word just before it. An example is done for you.

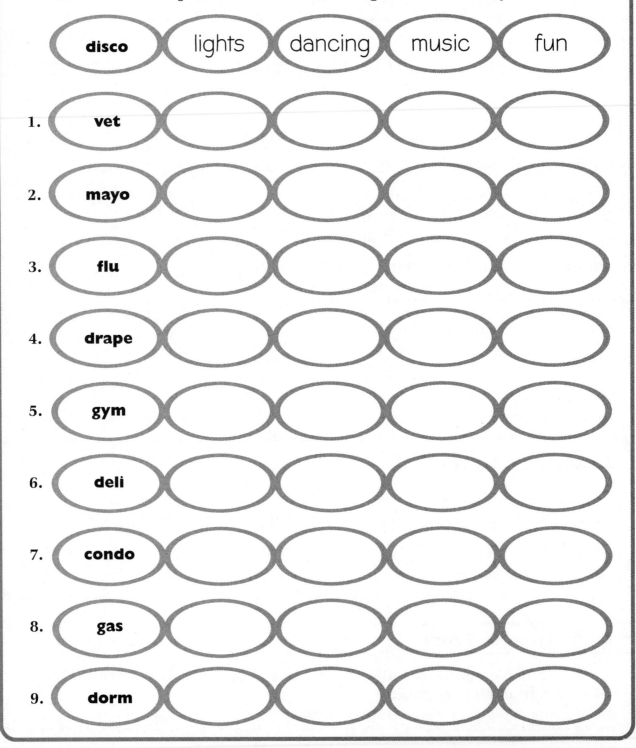

disco — lights — dancing — music — fun

1. vet
2. mayo
3. flu
4. drape
5. gym
6. deli
7. condo
8. gas
9. dorm

Blends

moped	smash	heliport	twirl	telecast
brunch	smog	cheeseburger	motel	chortle

▌A **BLEND** IS A WORD FORMED WHEN PARTS OF TWO
WORDS ARE COMBINED OR BLENDED TOGETHER.

A bicycle with a motor is a **moped**.

If you **smash** something, you shatter it.

Helicopters land and take off from a **heliport**.

When you **twirl**, you turn around.

Brunch is a meal that combines breakfast and lunch.

Smog is fog that is polluted. / A **cheeseburger** is a hamburger with cheese.

A **motel** is a hotel for motorists. / When you **chortle**, you laugh.

If you turn on the TV, you
can see a **telecast**.

A. Write the blend formed from each pair of words.

1. breakfast and lunch

_____

2. chuckle and snort

_____

3. twist and whirl

_____

4. motor and pedal

_____

5. helicopter and airport

_____

6. smack and mash

_____

7. smoke and fog

_____

8. television and broadcast

_____

B. Write a vocabulary word for each clue.

1. I'm a place to sleep. _____ **2.** I'm a popular food. _____

Blends

moped	smash	heliport	twirl	telecast
brunch	smog	cheeseburger	motel	chortle

A. Use what you know. Write the best word to complete each sentence.

1. We slept late on Saturday, so our first meal was _____ .

2. Heavy _____ hung over the city and made everything gray.

3. The driver stopped for the night at a _____ along the highway.

4. Alice let out a _____ as she watched the comedy.

5. Your _____ has a motor so it's not allowed on this walking path.

6. The pilot went to the _____ for his flight.

7. Scott likes his _____ on a toasted bun.

8. The autumn leaves spin and _____ as they flutter down.

9. You could hear the _____ of bottles when the bag broke.

10. The game will be _____ tonight at eight o'clock.

B. Read each question. Choose the best answer.

1. Which one is a vehicle? ❏ motel ❏ moped
2. Which one is a sound? ❏ smash ❏ smog
3. Which one can you see? ❏ telecast ❏ chortle
4. Which one is a meal? ❏ branch ❏ brunch

✏ Writing to Learn

Write a traffic report. Use at least two vocabulary words.

© 240 VOCABULARY WORDS FOR GRADE 4 SCHOLASTIC PROFESSIONAL BOOKS

Blends

Use the clues to complete the puzzle.

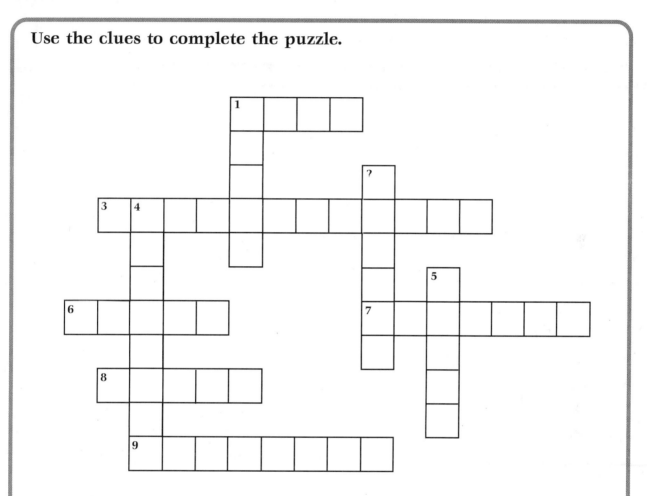

Across

1. more than fog

3. more than a hamburger

6. what a dancer does

7. a chuckle

8. more than a bike

9. on the air

Down

1. a noisy crash

2. more than breakfast

4. a pad for copters

5. a place to park and sleep

Content Words: Math

polygon	parallel	estimate	congruent	triangle
diameter	octagon	probability	diagonal	pentagon

SPECIAL WORDS NAME AND DESCRIBE LINES, FIGURES, AND FUNCTIONS IN **MATH**.

A **polygon** is a closed figure with three or more straight lines.

Parallel lines are always the same distance apart.

When you **estimate**, you make a careful guess about quantity.

When two figures are equal in size and shape, they are **congruent**.

A **diameter** is a straight line through the center of a circle.

An **octagon** is a figure with eight sides and eight angles.

Probability refers to the chances of something happening.

A line that slants is a **diagonal**.

A **pentagon** is a figure that has five sides and five angles.

A **triangle** is a figure with three sides and three angles.

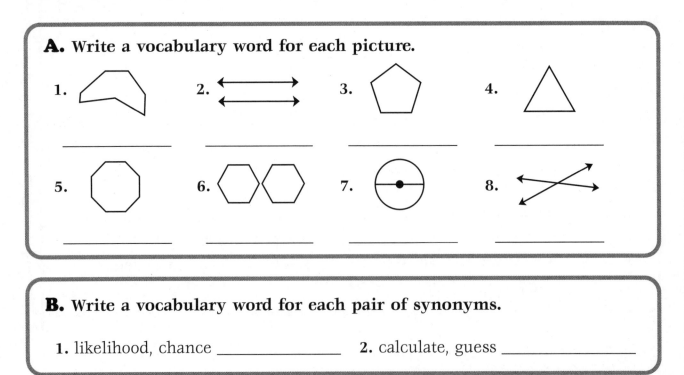

A. Write a vocabulary word for each picture.

1. _____   2. _____   3. _____   4. _____

5. _____   6. _____   7. _____   8. _____

B. Write a vocabulary word for each pair of synonyms.

1. likelihood, chance _____   2. calculate, guess _____

Content Words: Math

polygon	parallel	estimate	congruent	triangle
diameter	octagon	probability	diagonal	pentagon

A. Use what you know. Write the best word to complete each sentence.

1. Railroad tracks are _____ lines.

2. The class had to _____ how much food was needed for the party.

3. Instead of horizontal and vertical lines, the artist used _____ lines in his design.

4. According to the weather report, the _____ of rain is great.

5. The two shapes were identical and therefore were _____ .

6. A triangle, pentagon, and octagon are all examples of a _____ .

7. A building with eight sides is an _____ .

8. Tasha drew a five-pointed _____ .

9. The _____ divides the circle into halves.

10. The three stakes formed the points of a _____ .

B. Read each question. Choose the best answer.

1. Which one means "three"?   ❏ tri   ❏ penta
2. Which one means "eight"?   ❏ quadri   ❏ oct
3. Which one means "many"?   ❏ poly   ❏ para
4. Which one means "across"?   ❏ deca   ❏ dia

✎ Writing to Learn

Make up two math questions. Use at least one vocabulary word in each.

Content Words: Math

Use the vocabulary words to fill in the map. Then add other words that you know.

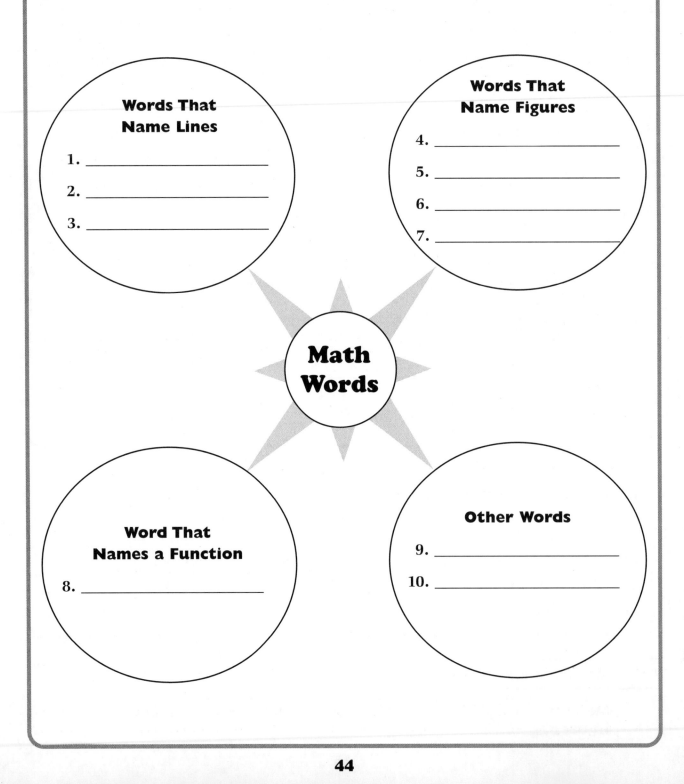

Words That Name Lines

1. _____
2. _____
3. _____

Words That Name Figures

4. _____
5. _____
6. _____
7. _____

Math Words

Word That Names a Function

8. _____

Other Words

9. _____
10. _____

Content Words: Animals

ram	stallion	cob	buck	billy
ewe	mare	pen	doe	nanny

MALE AND **FEMALE ANIMALS** OFTEN HAVE SPECIAL NAMES.

A male sheep is called a **ram.**

A female sheep is called a **ewe.**

A male horse is a **stallion,** and a female horse is a **mare.**

A **cob** is a male swan, while a **pen** is a female.

If you are speaking of a female deer, it's a **doe,** but a male deer is a **buck.**

You call a female goat a **nanny** and a male goat a **billy.**

A. Complete the chart.

Animal	Male	Female
deer	buck	1._____
sheep	2._____	ewe
horse	3._____	4._____
5._____	billy	nanny
6._____	cob	7._____

B. Answer the questions.

1. Does a buck or a doe have antlers? _____

2. Does a billy or a nanny give milk? _____

3. Does a ram or a ewe have lambs? _____

Content Words: Animals

ram	stallion	cob	buck	billy
ewe	mare	pen	doe	nanny

A. Use what you know. Write the best word to complete each sentence.

1. The white _____ lifted his wings as he came out of the water.

2. In the stable, a brown _____ put her head over the stall.

3. Once a year a _____ loses his antlers.

4. We watched as a _____ led her fawn across the lane.

5. The male sheep, called a _____ , is larger than the female.

6. Dairy goats give milk, and a _____ must be milked twice a day.

7. The _____ raced across the field with his tail and mane flowing.

8. A _____ gives birth to one or more lambs at a time.

9. The _____ hissed when we got too near her nest.

10. Like most goats, a _____ is likely to eat any plant he finds.

B. Read each question. Choose the best answer.

1. Which word also means "writing tool"?   ❑ pan   ❑ pen
2. Which word is a homophone?   ❑ ewe   ❑ ever
3. Which word is a homograph?   ❑ buck   ❑ luck
4. What's the antonym of billy?   ❑ goat   ❑ nanny

✍ Writing to Learn

Write a story about a visit to a farm. Use at least three vocabulary words in your story.

© 240 VOCABULARY WORDS FOR GRADE 4   SCHOLASTIC PROFESSIONAL BOOKS

Content Words: Animals

Use vocabulary words to fill in the map.

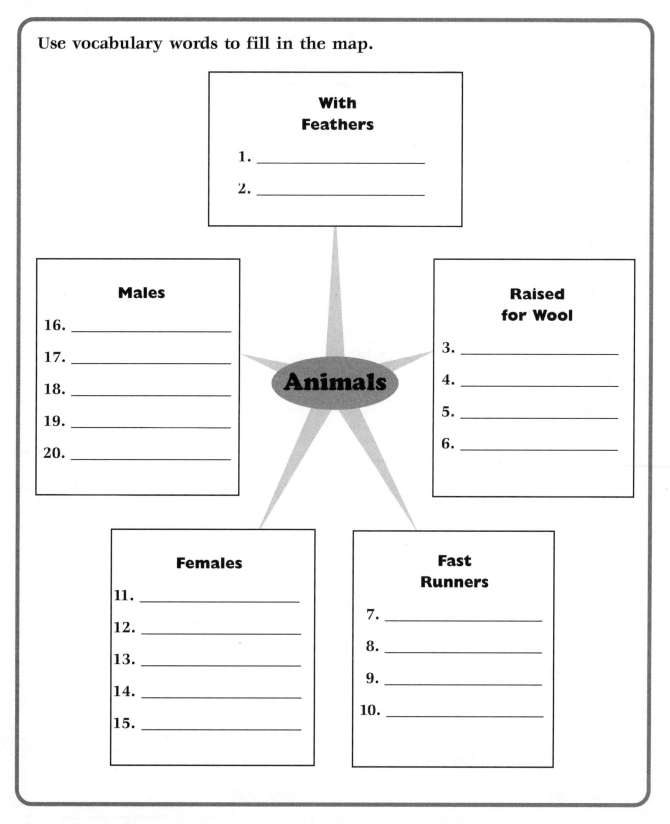

With Feathers

1. _____
2. _____

Males

16. _____
17. _____
18. _____
19. _____
20. _____

Raised for Wool

3. _____
4. _____
5. _____
6. _____

Animals

Females

11. _____
12. _____
13. _____
14. _____
15. _____

Fast Runners

7. _____
8. _____
9. _____
10. _____

Latin Roots *art, pop, corp*

artisan	artistic	population	popular	corporal
artifact	artist	populous	corporation	corps

MANY WORDS HAVE LATIN ROOTS.

A **corps** is a group of people with special training.

Root:

Art means "art."
An **artisan** is a craftsperson skilled in an industry or trade.

An **artifact** is something, such as a tool, made by human skill.

Artistic means "having to do with art or artists."

An **artist** is someone who paints or is skilled in other fine arts.

Pop means "people."
The **population** is the number of people living in a place.

When a place is **populous**, it has a lot of people.

If you are **popular**, you are well liked.

Corp means "body."
A **corporation** is an organization made up of a group of people who act as one.

Corporal means "having to do with the body."

A. Read the vocabulary word. Find and circle two other words that mean almost the same thing.

1. **popular**	favored	liked	detested
2. **artist**	arrow	painter	sculptor
3. **populous**	crowded	sparse	populated
4. **artistic**	creative	skilled	clumsy
5. **corporation**	corner	company	organization
6. **population**	people	popularity	inhabitants
7. **artifact**	tool	object	agent

B. Underline the root in each word.

1. **artisan**   2. **corps**   3. **corporal**

Latin Roots *art, pop, corp*

artisan	**art**istic	**pop**ulation	**pop**ular	**corp**oral
artifact	**art**ist	**pop**ulous	**corp**oration	**corp**s

A. Use what you know. Write the best word to complete each sentence.

1. Tokyo, Japan, is a crowded and _____ city.

2. The beautiful cabinets showed that the carpenter was a good _____ .

3. Justin's feelings were hurt, but he suffered no _____ harm.

4. Monet was a famous _____ , and his paintings hang in museums.

5. While digging near a stream, the scientists found a very old _____ .

6. Tracy's mother works for a large _____ .

7. That radio program is very _____ with teens.

8. Leon works with a _____ of students who clean up the park.

9. In the last ten years, the _____ of our town has doubled.

10. Kyle decorated the room in an _____ way.

B. Read each question. Choose the best answer.

1. Which word is an adjective? ❏ population   ❏ popular
2. Which word is a noun? ❏ artisan   ❏ artistic
3. Which word is a homophone? ❏ corporal   ❏ corporation
4. Which word is a homograph? ❏ car   ❏ corps

Writing to Learn

Explain why it is helpful to know the root of a word. Use at least two vocabulary words as your examples.

Latin Roots *art, pop, corp*

Read the clues. Then complete the puzzle.

1. amount of people in a place _____

2. relating to the body _____

3. showing talent in the arts _____

4. a skilled worker _____

5. a business organization _____

6. admired _____

7. a squad or team _____

8. packed with people _____

9. item made by people _____

10. a creator of art _____

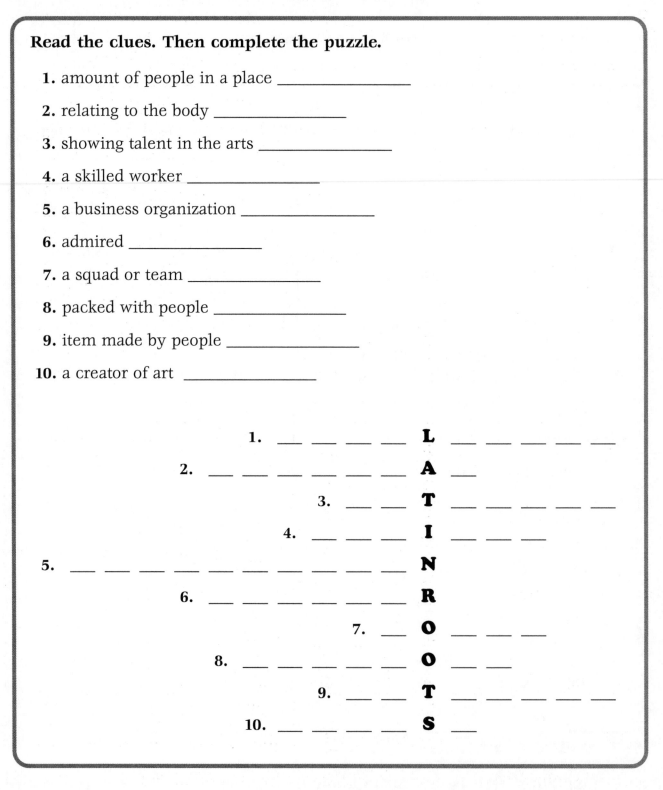

© 240 VOCABULARY WORDS FOR GRADE 4   SCHOLASTIC PROFESSIONAL BOOKS

Latin Roots *aqua, port*

aquarium	aquamarine	aqueduct	transport	comport
aquatic	aquanaut	portable	porter	report

MANY WORDS HAVE LATIN ROOTS.

An **aquanaut** is an underwater explorer.

Root:

Aqua means "water."

A tank for fish is called an **aquarium**.

Something that is **aquatic** is related to water.

Aquamarine is a blue-green color like water.

An **aqueduct** is a pipe or channel that carries water.

Port means "carry."

When something is easily moved from place to place, it is **portable**.

If you **transport** something, you take it from one place to another.

A **porter** is someone who carries baggage.

Comport means "the way you behave."

A **report** is an account prepared in an organized form.

A. Read each vocabulary word. Find and circle two other words that mean almost the same thing.

1. **comport**	act	behave	compost
2. **transport**	tramp	carry	tote
3. **aquarium**	bowl	arrangement	tank
4. **aqueduct**	pipe	approve	channel
5. **report**	resort	retelling	account
6. **aquatic**	wet	watery	action
7. **aquanaut**	diver	alligator	explorer

B. Underline the root in each word.

1. **aquamarine**   2. **portable**   3. **porter**

Latin Roots *aqua, port*

aquarium	**aqua**marine	**aque**duct	trans**port**	com**port**
aquatic	**aqua**naut	**port**able	**port**er	re**port**

A. Use what you know. Write the best word to complete each sentence.

1. When Grandpa arrived at the airport, a _____ helped him with his suitcase.

2. Everyone in the class will write a _____ about the field trip.

3. An _____ brings water to the villages in the valley.

4. I use a laptop computer when traveling because it's so _____ .

5. The students took turns feeding the fish in their _____ .

6. Large trucks _____ food to supermarkets all over the country.

7. The movie is about an _____ who works in an underwater station.

8. Vicki wore an _____ sweater with her jeans.

9. We learned about _____ plants that grow in the pond.

10. Mom asked my brother to _____ himself quietly in the library.

B. Read each question. Choose the best answer.

1. Which one could be a crayon?   ❏ aquanaut   ❏ aquamarine

2. Which one is portable?   ❏ tent   ❏ tower

3. What does a train do?   ❏ transport   ❏ transform

4. What does a newspaper do?   ❏ report   ❏ repay

✎ Writing to Learn

Write a dialogue between two people. Use at least two vocabulary words in your dialogue.

Latin Roots *aqua, port*

Play the So Is game. Complete each sentence with a vocabulary word.

1. Turquoise is a color and so is _____ .

2. A nest is a home and so is an _____ .

3. A tube is a pipe and so is an _____ .

4. An astronaut is an explorer and so is an _____ .

5. *Carry* is a word for "move things" and so is _____ .

6. An announcement is an account and so is a _____ .

7. A postal worker carries things and so does a _____ .

8. A frog is an _____ animal and so is a turtle.

9. A sleeping bag is _____ and so is a canteen.

10. *Behave* is a word for "how you act" and so is _____ .

NAME _____ DATE _____

Greek Word Parts *geo, photo, auto*

geography	geometry	photogenic	telephoto	autobiography
geology	photograph	photocopier	autograph	automatic

MANY WORDS CONTAIN GREEK WORD PARTS.

Lily Brooks

When you sign your name, you write your **autograph**.

Word Part:

Geo means "Earth."   The study of Earth's surface is called **geography**.
The science of how Earth was formed is called **geology**.
Geometry is the study of angles, lines, and figures.

Photo means "light."   A **photograph** is a picture taken by a camera.
Someone who is **photogenic** looks good in photographs.
A **photocopier** is a machine that makes copies.
A **telephoto** lens can take pictures at great distances.

Auto means "self."   If you write the story of your life, it's an **autobiography**.
Something that is **automatic** is self-propelled.

A. Draw a line to match each description with the correct vocabulary word.

1. a biography about yourself
2. a door that opens before you touch it
3. an image taken with the use of light
4. the study of rocks that make up Earth
5. a lens that receives light from far away
6. a signature that you write
7. a lesson in circles, squares, and triangles

a. **telephoto**
b. **geology**
c. **autograph**
d. **automatic**
e. **geometry**
f. **photograph**
g. **autobiography**

B. Underline the Greek word part in each vocabulary word.

1. **geography**   2. **photocopier**   3. **photogenic**

Greek Word Parts *geo, photo, auto*

geography	**geo**metry	**photo**genic	tele**photo**	**auto**biography
geology	**photo**graph	**photo**copier	**auto**graph	**auto**matic

A. Use what you know. Write the best word to complete each sentence.

1. The class learned about mountains and other landforms
   in _____ .

2. The movie star was very _____ and posed for many pictures.

3. The neighbors put in an _____ sprinkler system for their garden.

4. The students worked with cubes and spheres in _____ class.

5. These pictures of the countryside were taken with a _____ lens.

6. Bob asked the author to _____ her latest book.

7. Mr. Chee used the _____ to reproduce the minutes
   of the meeting.

8. A geologist is someone who studies _____ .

9. On the desk was a _____ of the whole family.

10. In his _____ , the singer told about his childhood.

B. Read each question. Choose the best answer.

1. Which one is a science? ❏ geology ❏ geometry
2. Which one is a book? ❏ automatic ❏ autobiography
3. Which one is a picture? ❏ photogenic ❏ photograph
4. Which one is a machine? ❏ photocopy ❏ photocopier

Writing to Learn

Explain how two of the vocabulary words were formed.

Greek Word Parts *geo, photo, auto*

Read the clues. Then find and circle each word in the puzzle. Write the word next to its clue.

```
A  C  X  P  H  O  T  O  G  E  N  I  C  D
U  E  S  P  M  G  E  O  M  E  T  R  Y  G
T  D  N  H  X  W  S  L  P  V  E  F  H  E
O  U  A  O  I  N  G  Q  P  B  L  J  Y  O
M  Z  U  T  A  F  E  W  M  X  E  O  C  G
A  U  T  O  B  I  O  G  R  A  P  H  Y  R
T  F  O  G  U  E  L  R  V  T  H  B  M  A
I  N  G  R  C  G  O  J  P  N  O  Y  H  P
C  X  R  A  Q  L  G  N  R  H  T  V  B  H
Q  I  A  P  D  S  Y  E  M  T  O  J  S  Y
K  S  P  H  O  T  O  C  O  P  I  E  R  N
A  O  H  Z  W  D  V  L  C  H  X  Q  C  U
```

1. looking great on film   _____

2. works by itself   _____

3. a life story   _____

4. study of lines and angles   _____

5. what a camera takes   _____

6. long distance view   _____

7. rocky subject   _____

8. study of land and sea   _____

9. handwritten name   _____

10. duplicating device   _____

Coined Words

astronaut	**suburb**	**hatchback**	**jazz**	**laptop**
skyscraper	**nylon**	**takeout**	**monorail**	**infomercial**

WHEN SOMETHING NEW IS INVENTED, IT NEEDS A NAME.
A MADE-UP NAME IS CALLED A **COINED WORD**.

An **astronaut** is the pilot of a spacecraft.

A community outside a large city is a **suburb**.

A car with a hatch in the back is a **hatchback**.

A **skyscraper** is a very tall building.

Jazz is music with strong rhythm and an accented beat that falls in unusual places.

A **laptop** is a small portable computer. / **Nylon** is a material made from chemicals.

Prepared food that you take home to eat is called **takeout**.

A **monorail** is a train that runs on a single track.

An **infomercial** is a TV program that gives information and also sells a product.

A. Write the correct vocabulary word for each picture.

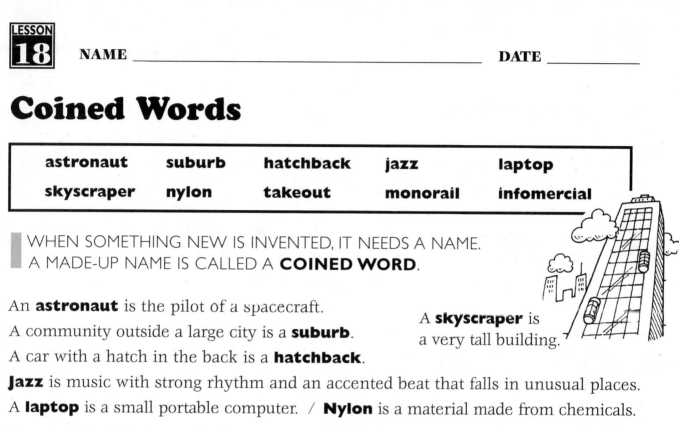

1. _____

2. _____

3. _____

4. _____

5. _____

6. _____

B. Read each group of words. Write the vocabulary word that best goes with each group.

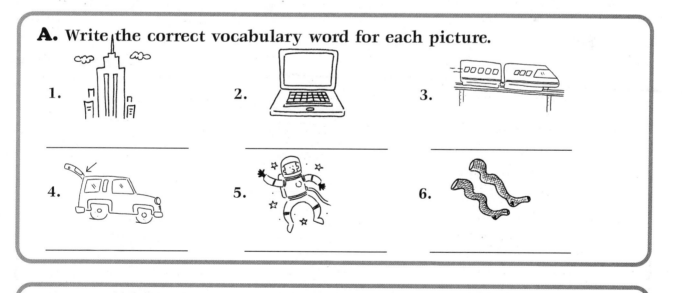

1. homes, cars, schools _____

2. trumpet, piano, saxophone _____

3. pizza, sushi, hamburger _____

4. jewelry, clothes, housewares _____

Coined Words

astronaut	suburb	hatchback	jazz	laptop
skyscraper	nylon	takeout	monorail	infomercial

A. Use what you know. Write the best word to complete each sentence.

1. In the parking lot, Mom loaded the groceries into the _____ .

2. Penny wore a _____ jacket when she went out.

3. From his spaceship, the _____ could see Earth.

4. The trio played _____ at the concert.

5. Mr. Farro's company was on the twentieth floor of the _____ .

6. Tim took his _____ so he could work on the plane.

7. After she saw the _____ , Mrs. Ford wanted to place an order.

8. Let's get _____ for dinner tonight.

9. Many people leave the _____ each day to work in the city.

10. A _____ carried people from one terminal to the other.

B. Read each question. Choose the best answer.

1. Which one has stories?   ❑ skyscraper   ❑ skylight
2. Which one is a vehicle?   ❑ hatchback   ❑ astronaut
3. Which one is nylon?   ❑ threat   ❑ thread
4. Which one is food?   ❑ takeover   ❑ takeout

✎ Writing to Learn

Draw a cartoon based on one of the vocabulary words. Use at least one other vocabulary word in the caption.

Coined Words

For each possible cause, write a vocabulary word that was a result.

CAUSE		RESULT
1. space program	⇨	_____
2. elevator	⇨	_____
3. population growth	⇨	_____
4. computer age	⇨	_____
5. television	⇨	_____
6. busy schedules	⇨	_____
7. ragtime and blues	⇨	_____
8. an amusement park ride	⇨	_____
9. experiments of a chemist	⇨	_____
10. demands of family chores	⇨	_____

Word Stories

panic	flashy	gargantuan	china	pineapple
vandalism	popcorn	jeep	funny bone	eavesdrop

MANY WORDS HAVE INTERESTING **STORIES** ABOUT THEIR ORIGINS.

If you **panic**, you have a sudden and unreasonable fear.

Something that is colorful and stands out is **flashy**.

China is a fine pottery used to make dishes.

A **pineapple** is a fruit that looks like a pinecone.

Vandalism means the destruction of valued things.

Popcorn is made by heating corn kernels.

A **jeep** is a powerful car with four-wheel drive.

The place where a nerve passes your bended elbow is called a **funny bone**.

When you **eavesdrop**, you listen in on someone's conversation.

Something that is **gargantuan** is huge.

A. Write a vocabulary word for each word story.

1. Dishes made of fine pottery first came from China. _____

2. When corn grains explode, they make a popping sound. _____

3. The name of a tropical fruit means "apple of the pine." _____

4. A General Purpose vehicle in the army was called a GP. _____

B. Draw a line from each vocabulary word to the person or place for which it is named.

1. **panic**   a. Gypsies who dressed in bright clothes lived in an English village called Flash.

2. **gargantuan**   b. A book by a French author was about a giant called Gargantua.

3. **flashy**   c. The ancient Greeks thought the god Pan made frightening noises in the woods.

© 240 VOCABULARY WORDS FOR GRADE 4   SCHOLASTIC PROFESSIONAL BOOKS

Word Stories

panic	flashy	gargantuan	china	pineapple
vandalism	popcorn	jeep	funny bone	eavesdrop

A. Use what you know. Write the best word to complete each sentence.

1. The singer wore a _____ shirt with spangles on it.

2. When Robin banged her elbow on the door, it hurt her _____ .

3. Dad always buys a bag of _____ at the movies.

4. The spy was trying to _____ on their conversations.

5. Scott drove the _____ easily along the muddy dirt road.

6. The guests ate off fine _____ at the formal dinner.

7. You have to cut open a _____ to get at the fruit.

8. The loud noise caused Barry to _____ .

9. The old building was a wreck because of _____ .

10. After the fierce storm, _____ piles of snow drifted around the house.

B. Read each question. Choose the best answer.

1. Which one do you notice? ❏ dull   ❏ flashy
2. Which one breaks?   ❏ china   ❏ chino
3. Which one is a crime?   ❏ vandalism ❏ vanilla
4. Which one is rude?   ❏ eastward ❏ eavesdrop

Writing to Learn

Find out more about the story behind one of the vocabulary words. Write a paragraph to explain its background.

Word Stories

Read each list of words. Write a vocabulary word to go with each group.

1. _____
   juicy
   cone
   sweet

2. _____
   fear
   terror
   alarm

3. _____
   gaudy
   showy
   dazzling

4. _____
   wreckage
   destruction
   ruin

5. _____
   huge
   enormous
   oversized

6. _____
   salty
   buttery
   tasty

7. _____
   porcelain
   pottery
   dishes

8. _____
   truck
   automobile
   vehicle

9. _____
   bone
   arm
   nerve

10. _____
    listen
    overhear
    pry

© 240 VOCABULARY WORDS FOR GRADE 4   SCHOLASTIC PROFESSIONAL BOOKS

NAME _____   DATE _____

Newspaper Jargon

dummy	beat	bleeds	widow	typo
masthead	scoop	crop	headline	stringer

The **headline** of a newspaper article is the title of the story.

▌ THE SPECIAL VOCABULARY USED BY PEOPLE WHO WORK AT CERTAIN JOBS IS CALLED **JARGON**.

A **dummy** is a model of how a page will look.

The area or subject that a reporter covers is called a **beat**.

When a picture goes to the edge of a page, it **bleeds**.

A **widow** is a word on a line by itself at the end of a paragraph.

A **typo** is a mistake in a printed word caused by hitting the wrong letter key.

The names of a newspaper's publishers and editors are listed on the **masthead**.

If a newspaper publishes a big story before anyone else, it's a **scoop**.

If you cut off part of a picture, you **crop** it.

A **stringer** is a reporter who is not on the newspaper staff but sends in stories.

A. Read the newspaper jargon word. Find and circle two other words that mean almost the same thing.

1. **dummy**	mock up	doll	model
2. **bleed**	injure	run	extend
3. **scoop**	first	precede	shovel
4. **typo**	error	compose	mistake
5. **crop**	plant	cut	trim
6. **beat**	assignment	specialty	attack
7. **stringer**	writer	journalist	twine

B. Write the newspaper jargon word for each clue.

1. a list of names _____   2. an extra word _____

Newspaper Jargon

dummy	beat	bleeds	widow	typo
masthead	scoop	crop	headline	stringer

A. Use what you know. Write the best word to complete each sentence.

1. The reporter's _____ was City Hall, and his story was about the mayor.

2. The editor wanted to focus on the boy's face so she decided to _____ the photo.

3. Clay's fingers flew over the keys, but he rarely made a _____ .

4. The _____ called to say she had a good story on a robbery.

5. Maya was so proud when her name was listed as an editor on the _____ .

6. The art director made up a _____ to show how the page would look.

7. The picture on this page will _____ across the margin.

8. Marie had some good contacts and got a _____ on a big story.

9. The _____ about the fire was in large bold type.

10. Cut a few words to get rid of the _____ at the end of the story.

B. Read each question. Choose the best answer.

1. Which one do you correct?   ❑ typo   ❑ type
2. Which one is first?   ❑ scoop   ❑ scope
3. Which one is extra?   ❑ window   ❑ widow
4. Which one is a stringer?   ❑ reader   ❑ reporter

Writing to Learn

Pretend you are a newspaper editor. Write a memo to your staff. Use at least three words in newspaper jargon.

Newspaper Jargon

Complete the chart. Write the jargon meaning for each word.

WORD	USUAL MEANING	NEWSPAPER JARGON
1. **bleed**	*lose blood*	_____
2. **headline**	*part of a body, and a long narrow mark*	_____
3. **scoop**	*a small shovel*	_____
4. **crop**	*plants grown by a farmer*	_____
5. **stringer**	*someone who hangs string*	_____
6. **dummy**	*a lifelike doll*	_____
7. **beat**	*hit*	_____
8. **masthead**	*a tall pole for a boat, and a part of the body*	_____
9. **widow**	*a woman whose husband has died*	_____

Funny Words

poppycock	bamboozle	polliwog	dillydally	bonkers
slugabed	scalawag	ballyhoo	hobnob	gobbledygook

SOME WORDS ARE FUN TO KNOW BECAUSE THEY SOUND OR LOOK **FUNNY**.

If there is an uproar about something, there is a lot of **ballyhoo**.

Poppycock means "nonsense."

When you **bamboozle** someone, you trick that person.

A **polliwog** is a tadpole—a frog in a very young stage.

If you **dillydally**, you waste time. / **Bonkers** means "crazy or mad."

Someone who is lazy is a **slugabed**. / A **scalawag** is a rascal or scamp.

If you **hobnob** with someone, you are on familiar terms with that person.

Gobbledygook is writing or speaking that is long and windy and hard to understand.

A. Read the words in each row. Cross out the word that does not have a similar meaning to the vocabulary word.

1. **bamboozle**	fool	bamboo	deceive
2. **dillydally**	linger	dawdle	rush
3. **poppycock**	popcorn	foolishness	rubbish
4. **bonkers**	calm	nuts	wild
5. **ballyhoo**	commotion	ballroom	disturbance
6. **scalawag**	scarecrow	troublemaker	good-for-nothing
7. **hobnob**	associate	hobble	know
8. **gobbledygook**	confusing	wordy	clear

B. Write a vocabulary word for each picture.

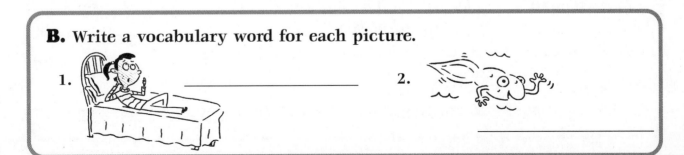

1. _____

2. _____

Funny Words

poppycock	bamboozle	polliwog	dillydally	bonkers
slugabed	scalawag	ballyhoo	hobnob	gobbledygook

A. Use what you know. Write the best word to complete each sentence.

1. The crowd went _____ when the home team won.

2. If you _____ over your meal, we'll miss the show.

3. Beware of deals that try to _____ you into parting with money.

4. A _____ has a tail but has not yet developed legs.

5. Gina waited by the stage door so she could _____ with the dancers.

6. The report was full of long, unclear sentences and _____ .

7. In the show, Arnie Piper plays a no-good character who is a _____ .

8. There was a _____ in town when the TV camera crew arrived.

9. Leah is a real _____ and has to be reminded of her chores.

10. Dina didn't believe the news and said it was a lot of _____ .

B. Read each question. Choose the best answer.

1. Which one's a slugabed?   ❏ sleepyhead   ❏ masthead
2. What happens when you dillydally? ❏ early   ❏ late
3. Who might bamboozle?   ❏ scalawag   ❏ polliwog
4. When do you go bonkers?   ❏ weary   ❏ excited

✒ Writing to Learn

Write a poem full of poppycock. Use at least two vocabulary words.

Funny Words

Answer each question. Have fun with your responses.

1. Why might you **dillydally**? _____
   _____

2. What might cause you to go **bonkers**? _____
   _____

3. When might you be a **slugabed**? _____
   _____

4. When might you write **gobbledygook**? _____
   _____

5. When might you **bamboozle** someone? _____
   _____

6. When might you give a **poppycock** answer? _____
   _____

7. What might you say to a **scalawag**? _____
   _____

8. How might you cause a **ballyhoo**? _____
   _____

9. With whom would you like to **hobnob**? _____
   _____

10. Where might you see a **polliwog**? _____
    _____

© 240 VOCABULARY WORDS FOR GRADE 4 SCHOLASTIC PROFESSIONAL BOOKS

NAME _____   DATE _____

Prefixes *super-, dis-, pre-, semi-, uni-*

supermarket	**dis**please	**pre**view	**semi**circle	**uni**cycle
superhuman	**dis**honest	**pre**historic	**semi**precious	**uni**corn

▌ A **PREFIX** IS A WORD PART THAT IS ADDED TO THE BEGINNING OF A WORD. A PREFIX CHANGES THE MEANING OF THE WORD.

super- means "more than"   *dis-* means "not; away"
pre- means "before"   *semi-* means "half"
uni- means "one"

Someone who is **superhuman** shows extra strength or power.

If you **displease** someone, you annoy that person.

A person who cheats or lies is **dishonest**.

If you get a **preview** of something, you see it in advance.

Prehistoric means "before recorded history."

A **semicircle** is half a circle. / **Semiprecious** jewels aren't as valuable as real ones.

A **unicycle** has one wheel.

A **unicorn** is an imaginary animal with one horn on its forehead.

A **supermarket** is a large food store.

A. Add the correct prefix to each word to form a new word. Use the meaning clue in parentheses to help you.

1. (before) _____ view

2. (one) _____ cycle

3. (not) _____ please

4. (half) _____ precious

5. (more than) _____ human

6. (more than) _____ market

B. Write the correct word to complete each sentence. Use the picture clues to help you.

1. I am _____ .

2. I am a _____ .

3. I am _____ .

4. I am a _____ .

Prefixes *super-, dis-, pre-, semi-, uni-*

supermarket	**dis**please	**pre**view	**semi**circle	**uni**cycle
superhuman	**dis**honest	**pre**historic	**semi**precious	**uni**corn

A. Use what you know. Write the best word to complete each sentence.

1. It took _____ effort for the men to push the truck off the road.

2. Historic events that happened long ago before there was written language are _____ .

3. Did the missing wallet mean a _____ person was in the room?

4. The clown balanced very well as he rode around on a _____ .

5. Jenna had a gold ring with a _____ stone in it.

6. We are going to see a _____ of the play before it officially opens.

7. The students sat in a _____ in front of the teacher.

8. After work, Mom will stop at the _____ to pick up food for dinner.

9. That's my dog's favorite chair, and it will _____ him if you sit there.

10. The painting showed the make-believe _____ running through a forest.

B. Read each question. Choose the best answer.

1. Which one is for beginners?   ❏ tricycle   ❏ unicycle
2. Which one happens first?   ❏ review   ❏ preview
3. Which one isn't complete?   ❏ semisoft   ❏ semicircle
4. Which one is dishonest?   ❏ fact   ❏ fib

Writing to Learn

Design a poster based on one of the vocabulary words. Use at least one other vocabulary word on the poster.

NAME _____   DATE _____

Prefixes *super-, dis-, pre-, semi-, uni-*

Underline the prefix in each word below. Use what you know about the prefix meaning to write the meaning of the word. Check your answers in a dictionary.

1. semicolon   _____

_____

2. disinterest   _____

_____

3. unicolor   _____

_____

4. superhighway   _____

_____

5. prejudge   _____

_____

6. semifinal   _____

_____

7. supertanker   _____

_____

8. prepaid   _____

_____

9. discolor   _____

_____

10. universe   _____

_____

Prefixes *non-, en-, multi-, post-, trans-*

nonfiction	**en**rage	**multi**colored	**post**date	**trans**continental
nonstop	**en**danger	**multi**purpose	**post**script	**trans**plant

▌ A **PREFIX** IS A WORD PART THAT IS ADDED TO THE BEGINNING OF A WORD.
A PREFIX CHANGES THE MEANING OF THE WORD.

non- means "not"   *en-* means "to cause"
multi- means "many"   *post-* means "after"
trans- means "across"

Nonfiction books are about real people and events.

When you travel **nonstop**, you don't stop along the way.

If you make someone really angry, you **enrage** that person.

By putting someone in harm's way, you **endanger** that person.

Something **multicolored** has many colors. / A **multipurpose** tool has many uses.

If you **postdate** something, you give a date later than the true date.

A **postscript** is added to the end of a letter after the signature.

Transcontinental means "across the continent."

When you **transplant** something, you move it from one place to another.

A. Add the correct prefix to each word to form a new word. Use the meaning clue in parentheses to help you.

1. (to cause) _____ rage

2. (not) _____ stop

3. (after) _____ date

4. (many) _____ purpose

5. (across) _____ continental

6. (after) _____ script

B. Write the correct word to complete each sentence. Use the picture clues to help you.

1. I am _____ .

2. We are _____ .

3. They will _____ me.

4. I can _____ you.

Prefixes non-, en-, multi-, post-, trans-

nonfiction	**en**rage	**multi**colored	**post**date	**trans**continental
nonstop	**en**danger	**multi**purpose	**post**script	**trans**plant

A. Use what you know. Write the best word to complete each sentence.

1. The initials P.S. at the end of a letter stand for __ _____ .

2. The gardener will _____ these flowers in the spring.

3. Dad wanted a _____ vehicle to fill all the needs of his business.

4. Look in the _____ section of the library for an encyclopedia.

5. Don't tease the bull, or you will _____ him.

6. Mrs. Field wore a _____ dress to the wedding.

7. The ambulance drove _____ to the hospital.

8. The newspaper is printed at night so they _____ it for the next day.

9. We took a _____ car trip across the country last summer.

10. The hole in that railing on the bridge could _____ many lives.

B. Read each question. Choose the best answers.

1. Which one is a biography?   ❏ fiction   ❏ nonfiction
2. Which one can you transplant?   ❏ heart   ❏ health
3. Which one is multicolored?   ❏ flour   ❏ flower
4. Which one has a postscript?   ❏ postcard   ❏ playing cards

✍ Writing to Learn

Explain how a prefix changes the meaning of a word. Use at least two vocabulary words as examples.

Prefixes *non-, en-, multi-, post-, trans-*

Here's a challenge for you. Write at least four words that begin with
each prefix. Use one of the words from each group in a sentence.

1. *multi-* _____

_____   _____

_____   _____

_____

2. *post-* _____

_____   _____

_____   _____

_____

3. *trans-* _____

_____   _____

_____   _____

_____

4. *en-* _____

_____   _____

_____   _____

_____

5. *non-* _____

_____   _____

_____   _____

_____

© 240 VOCABULARY WORDS FOR GRADE 4   SCHOLASTIC PROFESSIONAL BOOKS

Suffixes *-ship, -able, -ous, -hood, -ty*

kinship	**remarkable**	**envious**	**brotherhood**	**frailty**
leadership	**profitable**	**joyous**	**neighborhood**	**royalty**

▌ A **SUFFIX** IS A WORD PART THAT IS ADDED TO THE END OF A WORD.
A SUFFIX CHANGES THE MEANING OF THE WORD.

-ship and *-ty* mean "condition of being"   *-ous* means "full of"
-able means "that can be"   *-hood* means "a state of being"

Kinship means "related by blood."   **Royalty** means
Someone who is a good leader shows **leadership**.   "being royal."
Remarkable means "special."
If something is **profitable**, you make money on it.
If you are **envious**, you want what someone else has.
When you are happy, you are **joyous**. / **Brotherhood** means "fellowship."
A **neighborhood** is an area in a community. / **Frailty** is weakness.

A. Read the vocabulary word. Find and underline two other words in
the row that mean almost the same thing.

1. **remarkable**	extraordinary	uncommon	regular
2. **envious**	desiring	generous	jealous
3. **kinship**	relation	family	kindling
4. **frailty**	favor	feebleness	fragility
5. **profitable**	money-making	loss	prosperous
6. **joyous**	journalist	glad	cheerful
7. **royalty**	kingliness	monarchy	citizen
8. **brotherhood**	friendship	enemy	fellowship

B. Underline the suffix in each word.

1. **leadership**   2. **neighborhood**

Suffixes -ship, -able, -ous, -hood, -ty

kin**ship**	remark**able**	envi**ous**	brother**hood**	frail**ty**
leader**ship**	profit**able**	joy**ous**	neighbor**hood**	royal**ty**

A. Use what you know. Write the best word to complete each sentence.

1. After so many years, the childhood friends had a _____ reunion.

2. Some people are unhappy with the _____ of our state government.

3. It was an amazing and _____ story.

4. The _____ among the cousins was very strong.

5. The owner hoped her new business would soon be _____ .

6. We know almost all of the people who live in our _____ .

7. The prince walked proudly as did other members of the _____ .

8. Greg was discontented and _____ when his classmates were chosen for the team.

9. The kitten's _____ made it difficult for it to stand very long.

10. The students sang of _____ toward the people they supported.

B. Read each question. Choose the best answer.

1. Which one has street signs?   ❏ brotherhood   ❏ neighborhood
2. Which one is royalty?   ❏ princess   ❏ principal
3. What does a country need?   ❏ lectureship   ❏ leadership
4. Which one might be envious?   ❏ giver   ❏ taker

Writing to Learn

Pretend you are a king or queen. Write a royal greeting to your subjects. Use at least two vocabulary words.

Suffixes *-ship, -able, -ous, -hood, -ty*

Underline the suffix in each word below. Use what you know about the suffix meaning to write a sentence with the word. Check your answers in a dictionary.

1. adventurous _____

_____

2. sisterhood _____

_____

3. comfortable _____

_____

4. partnership _____

_____

5. loyalty _____

_____

6. authorship _____

_____

7. safety _____

_____

8. glamorous _____

_____

9. lovable _____

_____

10. childhood _____

_____

Word List

Answers

Lesson 1, page 6: A. 1. joy, happiness, gladness 2. name, choose, select 3. conquest, success, victory 4. alarm, surprise, shock 5. unhappiness, sorrow, regret 6. shaky, nervous, uneasy 7. amuse, frolic, play **B.** 1. pledge 2. sweltering 3. vessel **page 7: A.** 1. romp 2. vessel 3. appoint 4. triumph 5. sweltering 6. pledge 7. glee 8. jittery 9. grief 10. startle **B.** 1. ledge 2. park 3. pool 4. first **page 8:** Synonyms: glee/delight, appoint/choose; vessel/ship, victory/triumph, surprise/startle, play/romp, sorrow/grief, sweltering/steamy, pledge/promise, jittery/jumpy. **Riddle answer:** *umbrella*

Lesson 2, page 9: A. 1. unfurl 2. fret 3. din 4. chide 5. nimble 6. thaw 7. garment **B.** 1. nice 2. vest 3. lose **page 10: A.** 1. vast 2. unfurl 3. garment 4. trophy 5. chide 6. thaw 7. din 8. nimble 9. fret 10. eerie **B.** 1. spring 2. clatter 3. petals 4. garment **page 11:** 1. eerie 2. fret 3. chide 4. garment 5. nimble 6. vast 7. trophy 8. din 9. unfurl 10. thaw

Lesson 3, page 12: A. 1. relaxed 2. different 3. native 4. reveal 5. magnify 6. alike 7. alien **B.** 1. stirred, calm 2. appear, leave 3. decrease, enlarge **page 13: A.** 1. enlarge 2. identical 3. foreign 4. calm 5. dissimilar 6. appear 7. excited 8. native 9. reduce 10. vanish **B.** 1. Italian 2. twins 3. excited 4. subtraction **page 14:** vanish, foreign, enlarge, excited, identical

Lesson 4, page 15: A. 1. e 2. c 3. a 4. b 5. f 6. d **B.** 1. b. antonym, a. synonym 2. c. antonym, b. synonym 3. c. antonym, a. synonym 4. c. antonym, b. synonym **page 16: A.** 1. release 2. methodical 3. collect 4. torrent 5. snare 6. haphazard 7. trickle 8. disperse 9. maintain 10. discontinue **B.** 1. trap 2. haphazard 3. milk 4. collect **page 17:** 1. keep, maintain, preserve 2. distribute, scatter, disperse 3. careless, haphazard, unorganized 4. dribble, trickle, drip 5. snare, trap, capture

Lesson 5, page 18: A. 1. quicksand 2. beanstalk 3. textbook 4. waterfront 5. driftwood 6. sunburn 7. junkyard **B.** 1. land, mark 2. card, board 3. ginger, bread **page 19: A.** 1. sunburn 2. cardboard 3. quicksand 4. textbook 5. driftwood 6. waterfront 7. gingerbread 8. beanstalk 9. junkyard 10. landmark **B.** 1. beanstalk 2. landmark 3. sunburn 4. junkyard **page 20:** 1. textbook 2. sunburn 3. waterfront 4. quicksand 5. landmark 6. gingerbread 7. beanstalk 8. cardboard 9. junkyard 10. driftwood

Lesson 6, page 21: A. 1. boulder 2. sweet 3. boar 4. metal **B.** 1. vein 2. vain **page 22: A.** 1. suite 2. boulder 3. mettle 4. vain 5. sweet 6. bolder 7. metal 8. bore 9. veins 10. boar **B.** 1. gumdrop 2. spoon 3. bore 4. rock **page 23:** 1. The Vain Bore 2. Bolder Ways to Cook Sweet Food 3. Working with Metal 4. Your Veins and You 5. Decorating a Suite with Bolder Colors 6. The Boar Adventure: A Story of Real Mettle

Lesson 7, page 24: A. 1. a 2. a 3. a 4. b 5. b 6. b **B.** 1. prune 2. grouse 3. grouse 4. prune **page 25: A.** 1. desert 2. prune 3. grouse 4. desert 5. sewer 6. bass 7. bass 8. grouse 9. sewer 10. prune **B.** 1. no 2. no 3. yes 4. yes **page 26:** 1. a large underground channel; a person who uses a needle and thread 2. a plump bird; to grumble and fuss 3. a dry region; to flee from something 4. a fish that is good to eat; a drum with a low tone 5. to cut back plants; a dried fruit

Lesson 8, page 27: A. 1. sandwich 2. limerick 3. saxophone 4. Ferris wheel 5. guppy 6. braille **B.** 1. c 2. d 3. b 4. a **page 28: A.** 1. tweed 2. jovial 3. braille 4. limerick 5. bloomers 6. saxophone 7. sandwich 8. guppy 9. titanic 10. Ferris wheel **B.** 1. winner 2. tweed 3. guppy 4. sandwich **page 29:** 1. saxophone 2. limerick 3. titanic 4. tweed 5. braille 6. sandwich 7. jovial 8. bloomers 9. Ferris wheel 10. guppy

Lesson 9, page 30: A. 1. Dutch 2. Danish 3. Dutch 4. Danish 5. Dutch 6. Dutch 7. Spanish 8. Spanish **B.** 1. patio 2. rodeo **page 31: A.** 1. skull 2. caboose 3. sleigh 4. avocado 5. waffle 6. mustang 7. ski 8. yacht 9. rodeo 10. patio **B.** 1. avocado 2. caboose 3. skis 4. rodeo **page 32: Possible answers:** 1. Both provide protection by covering something. 2. relax, eat 3. They glide on runners on the snow. 4. They're both foods. 5. They are both used for having fun and going places. 6. A mustang is a horse; horses are ridden at rodeos. 7. They are both forms of transportation. 8. At a meal; it might grow there. 9. A mustang has a skull. 10. It might be part of a meal.

Lesson 10, page 33: A. 1. Malay 2. Italian 3. Japanese 4. Italian 5. French 6. Italian 7. Japanese 8. Italian **B.** 1. paddy 2. corduroy **page 34: A.** 1. futon 2. umbrella 3. gong 4. trampoline 5. judo 6. opera 7. paddy 8. corduroy 9. depot 10. ravioli **B.** 1. bong 2. puddle 3. depot 4. tumbling **page 35:** 1. opera 2. futon 3. trampoline 4. umbrella 5. depot 6. ravioli 7. judo 8. gong 9. corduroy 10. paddy

Lesson 11, page 36: A. 1. f 2. e 3. a 4. g 5. c 6. b 7. d **B.** 1. mayo 2. dorm 3. flu **page 37: A.** 1. dorm 2. mayo 3. drape 4. deli 5. gym 6. flu 7. gas 8. condo 9. vet 10. disco **B.** 1. condo 2. flu 3. vet 4. shop **page 38:** 1–9: Answers will vary.

Lesson 12, page 39: A. 1. brunch 2. chortle 3. twirl 4. moped 5. heliport 6. smash 7. smog 8. telecast **B.** 1. motel 2. cheeseburger **page 40: A.** 1. brunch 2. smog 3. motel 4. chortle 5. moped 6. heliport 7. cheeseburger 8. twirl 9. smash 10. telecast **B.** 1. moped 2. smash 3. telecast 4. brunch **page 41:** Across: 1. smog 3. cheeseburger 6. twirl 7. chortle 8. moped 9. telecast Down: 1. smash 2. brunch 4. heliport 5. motel

Lesson 13, page 42: A. 1. polygon 2. parallel 3. pentagon 4. triangle 5. octagon 6. congruent 7. diameter 8. diagonal **B.** 1. probability 2. estimate **page 43: A.** 1. parallel 2. estimate 3. diagonal 4. probability 5. congruent 6. polygon 7. octagon 8. pentagon 9. diameter 10. triangle **B.** 1. tri 2. oct 3. poly 4. dia **page 44:** Lines: 1. diagonal 2. parallel 3. diameter Figures: 4. polygon 5. octagon 6. triangle 7. pentagon Function: 8. estimate Other: 9. probability 10. congruent

Lesson 14, page 45: A. 1. doe 2. ram 3. stallion 4. mare 5. goat 6. swan 7. pen **B.** 1. buck 2. nanny 3. ewe **page 46: A.** 1. cob 2. mare 3. buck 4. doe 5. ram 6. nanny 7. stallion 8. ewe 9. pen 10. billy **B.** 1. pen 2. ewe 3. buck 4. nanny **page 47:** Feathers: 1-2. cob, pen Wool:3.-6. billy, nanny, ewe, ram Fast Runners: 7-10. buck, doe, stallion, mare Females: 11-15. ewe, mare, pen, nanny, doe Males: 16-20. buck, stallion, ram, billy, cob

Lesson 15, page 48: A. 1. favored, liked 2. painter, sculptor 3. crowded, populated 4. creative, skilled 5. company, organization 6. people, inhabitants 7. tool, object **B.** 1. artisan 2. corps 3. corporal **page 49: A.** 1. populous 2. artisan 3. corporal 4. artist 5. artifact 6. corporation 7. popular 8. corps 9. population 10. artistic **B.** 1. popular 2. artisan 3. corporal 4. corps **page 50:** 1. population 2. corporal 3. artistic 4. artisan 5. corporation 6. popular 7. corps 8. populous 9. artifact 10. artist

Lesson 16, page 51: A. 1. act, behave 2. carry, tote 3. bowl, tank 4. pipe, channel 5. retelling, account 6. wet, watery 7. diver, explorer **B.** 1. aquamarine 2. portable 3. porter **page 52: A.** 1. porter 2. report 3. aqueduct 4. portable 5. aquarium 6. transport 7. aquanaut 8. aquamarine 9. aquatic 10. comport **B.** 1. aquamarine 2. tent 3. transport 4. report **page 53:** 1. aquamarine 2. aquarium 3. aqueduct 4. aquanaut 5. transport 6. report 7. porter 8. aquatic 9. portable 10. comport

Lesson 17, page 54: A. 1. g 2. d 3. f 4. b 5. a 6. c 7. e **B.** 1. geography 2. photocopier 3. photogenic **page 55: A.** 1. geography 2. photogenic 3. automatic 4. geometry 5. telephoto 6. autograph 7. photocopier 8. geology 9. photograph 10. autobiography **B.** 1. geology 2. autobiography 3. photograph 4. photocopier **page 56:** 1. photogenic 2. automatic 3. autobiography 4. geometry 5. photograph 6. telephoto 7. geology 8. geography 9. autograph 10. photocopier

Lesson 18, page 57: A. 1. skyscraper 2. laptop 3. monorail 4. hatchback 5. astronaut 6. nylon **B.** 1. suburb 2. jazz 3. takeout 4. infomercial **page 58: A.** 1. hatchback 2. nylon 3. astronaut 4. jazz 5. skyscraper 6. laptop 7. infomercial 8. takeout 9. suburbs 10. monorail **B.** 1. skyscraper 2. hatchback 3. thread 4. takeout **page 59:** 1. astronaut 2. skyscraper 3. suburb 4. laptop 5. infomercial 6. takeout 7. jazz 8. monorail 9. nylon 10. hatchback

Lesson 19, page 60: A. 1. china 2. popcorn 3. pineapple 4. jeep **B.** 1. c 2. b 3. a **page 61: A.** 1. flashy 2. funny bone 3. popcorn 4. eavesdrop 5. jeep 6. china 7. pineapple 8. panic 9. vandalism 10. gargantuan **B.** 1. flashy 2. china 3. vandalism 4. eavesdrop **page 62:** 1. pineapple 2. panic 3. flashy 4. vandalism 5. gargantuan 6. popcorn 7. china 8. jeep 9. funny bone 10. eavesdrop

Lesson 20, page 63: A. 1. mockup, model 2. run, extend 3. first, precede 4. error, mistake 5. cut, trim 6. assignment, specialty 7. writer, journalist **B.** 1. masthead 2. widow **page 64: A.** 1. beat 2. crop 3. typo 4. stringer 5. masthead 6. dummy 7. bleed 8. scoop 9. headline 10. widow **B.** 1. typo 2. scoop 3. widow 4. reporter **page 65:** 1. extend a photo to the edge of the page 2. title of a newspaper story 3. a story published before other newspapers print it 4. to cut off part of a picture 5. a reporter who sends in stories but is not on staff 6. a model of a page before it's printed 7. a reporter's assigned area 8. list of publisher and editors 9. word on a line by itself at the end of a paragraph

Lesson 21, page 66: A. 1. bamboo 2. rush 3. popcorn 4. calm 5. ballroom 6. scarecrow 7. hobble 8. clear **B.** 1. slugabed 2. polliwog **page 67: A.** 1. bonkers 2. dillydally 3. bamboozle 4. polliwog 5. hobnob 6. gobbledygook 7. scalawag 8. ballyhoo 9. slugabed 10. poppycock **B.** 1. sleepyhead 2. late 3. scalawag 4. excited **page 68:** 1-10: Answers will vary.

Lesson 22, page 69: A. 1. preview 2. unicycle 3. displease 4. semiprecious 5. superhuman 6. supermarket **B.** 1. prehistoric 2. unicorn 3. dishonest 4. semicircle **page 70: A.** 1. superhuman 2. prehistoric 3. dishonest 4. unicycle 5. semiprecious 6. preview 7. semicircle 8. supermarket 9. displease 10. unicorn **B.** 1. tricycle 2. preview 3. semicircle 4. fib **page 71:** 1. semicolon; punctuation mark indicating a pause greater than a comma and less than a colon 2. disinterest; lack of interest 3. unicolor; all the same color 4. superhighway; large highway with six or more lanes 5. prejudge; make a judgment before knowing all the facts 6. semifinal; competition just before the final one 7. supertanker; large vessel for transporting oil 8. prepaid; paid before delivery 9. discolor; to stain or change the color of something 10. universe; the earth and all existing things

Lesson 23, page 72: A. 1. enrage 2. nonstop 3. postdate 4. multipurpose 5. transcontinental 6. postscript **B.** 1. nonfiction 2. multicolored 3. transplant 4. endanger **page 73: A.** 1. postscript 2. transplant 3. multipurpose 4. nonfiction 5. enrage 6. multicolored 7. nonstop 8. postdate 9. transcontinental 10. endanger **B.** 1. nonfiction 2. heart 3. flower 4. postcard **page 75:** 1-5: Answers will vary.

Lesson 24, page 75: A. 1. extraordinary, uncommon 2. desiring, jealous 3. relation, family 4. feebleness, fragility 5. money-making, prosperous 6. glad, cheerful 7. kingliness, monarchy 8. friendship, fellowship **B.** 1. leadership 2. neighborhood **page 76: A.** 1. joyous 2. leadership 3. remarkable 4. kinship 5. profitable 6. neighborhood 7. royalty 8. envious 9. frailty 10. brotherhood **B.** 1. neighborhood 2. princess 3. leadership 4. taker **page 77:** 1-10: Answers will vary.